Information Technology in Contemporary Organizations

Due to tremendous shifts in the business environment of contemporary organizations following the COVID-19 pandemic, there is a need to redefine the role and importance of information technology (IT) support, which is essential for ensuring an organization's survival. Current models are no longer valid, as in the new turbulent and digitalized environment, the need for IT support is more crucial and indispensable than ever. This book proposes a new model explaining the factors influencing the efficiency of adaptable IT support in contemporary organizations, including those operating normally and during crises.

The author demonstrates how organizations benefit from IT support, not only by enabling higher performance but also by facilitating organizational continuity, reliability, and even survival during various stages of crisis. The proposed model provides a basis for theory development in the field of organizational continuity and reliability, offering a new body of knowledge related to the factors boosting organizational performance gained from IT support and enabling organizational survival.

This book will provide valuable findings for scholars performing research in the field of IT use in organizations, IT management, crisis management, and organizational reliability.

Katarzyna Tworek is the Dean of the Faculty of Management at Wrocław University of Science and Technology, Poland. Her research interests include Information Technology, IT Management, Organizational Reliability, and Human Resource Management.

RIOT!

Routledge Studies in Innovation, Organizations and Technology

Public Innovation and Digital Transformation
Edited by Hannele Väyrynen, Nina Helander and Harri Jalonen

Innovation and Leadership in the Public Sector
The Australian Experience
Mahmoud Moussa, Leonie Newnham, Adela McMurray and Nuttawuth Muenjohn

Advancing Big Data Analytics for Healthcare Service Delivery
Tiko Iyamu

Open Labs and Innovation Management
The Dynamics of Communities and Ecosystems
Edited by Valérie Mérindol and David W. Versailles

Technology Brands in the Digital Economy
Edited by Wioleta Kucharska and Ewa Lechman

Business Models for Industry 4.0
Concepts and Challenges in SME Organizations
Sandra Grabowska and Sebastian Saniuk

Innovation in the Digital Economy
New Approaches to Management for Industry 5.0
Edited by Agnieszka Rzepka

Information Technology in Contemporary Organizations
Redefining IT Management for Organizational Reliability
Katarzyna Tworek

For more information about this series, please visit: www.routledge.com/Routledge-Studies-in-Innovation-Organizations-and-Technology/book-series/RIOT

Information Technology in Contemporary Organizations

Redefining IT Management for Organizational Reliability

Katarzyna Tworek

Routledge
Taylor & Francis Group
LONDON AND NEW YORK

First published 2023
by Routledge
4 Park Square, Milton Park, Abingdon, Oxon OX14 4RN

and by Routledge
605 Third Avenue, New York, NY 10158

Routledge is an imprint of the Taylor & Francis Group, an informa business

British Library Cataloguing-in-Publication Data
A catalogue record for this book is available from the British Library

ISBN: 978-1-032-42951-9 (hbk)
ISBN: 978-1-032-42952-6 (pbk)
ISBN: 978-1-003-36504-4 (ebk)

DOI: 10.4324/9781003365044

Typeset in Bembo
by codeMantra

Contents

List of figures ix
List of tables xi
Acknowledgments xiii

Introduction 1

1 IT use in contemporary organizations 6
1.1 IT in organizations 6
1.1.1 IT – definition 6
1.1.2 IT importance for organizations 8
1.1.2.1 IT deployment 9
1.1.2.2 IT-business alignment 9
1.1.2.3 Perceived usefulness of IT support 10
1.1.3 IT in organization – typology 12
1.1.4 IT life cycle 14
1.1.5 IT adoption models and IT success models 16
1.1.5.1 TAM model 17
1.1.5.2 PRECEDE model 19
1.1.5.3 IT success model 20
1.1.6 The need for a new model for IT use 20
1.2 Crisis as a cause for change of the perspective on IT 22
1.2.1 Crisis typologies 23
1.2.1.1 Conventional crisis: predictable, sensitive to influence, with well-known influence possibilities 24
1.2.1.2 Unexpected crisis: unpredictable, sensitive to influence 24
1.2.1.3 Intractable crisis: predictable, not sensitive to influence 25
1.2.1.4 Fundamental crisis: unpredictable, not sensitive to influence 25
1.2.2 BSE as a specific type of crisis 26
1.2.2.1 Crisis caused by BSE – research perspective 26
1.2.2.2 Crisis caused by BSE – stages 28
1.2.2.3 Crisis management in various crisis stage 30
1.2.3 COVID-19 as a specific example of Black Swan event 31

1.3 IT in crisis 33

1.3.1 IT during crisis caused by BSE 35

1.3.2 IT during crisis caused by specific BSE – the COVID-19 pandemic 35

1.3.3 IT after the COVID-19 pandemic 39

1.4 New understanding of IT support after BSE – the COVID-19 pandemic 39

2 EDC-enabled IT adaptability model of organizational performance 52

2.1 IT adaptability influence on organizational performance 52

2.2 IT adaptability 52

2.2.1 IT adaptability during BSE 57

2.2.2 IT adaptability, job performance, and organizational performance 59

2.2.2.1 Organizational performance and job performance – definition 60

2.2.2.2 IT adaptability influence on organizational performance through job performance 60

2.2.3 Boosters of IT adaptability influence on organizational performance 63

2.2.3.1 IT reliability as a booster 64

2.2.3.2 Organizational attitudes toward IT adaptability as a booster 67

2.2.3.3 Employees' attitudes toward IT adaptability as a booster 70

2.2.4 IT adaptability mediated influence on organizational performance 72

2.2.5 EDC as an enabler of IT adaptability 73

2.2.6 Model in crisis 77

3 Empirical research and model verification 86

3.1 Research methodology 86

3.2 Sample selection 87

3.3 Variables – scales reliability and validity 88

3.4 Regression analysis 90

3.5 Multigroup path analysis 91

3.5.1 Model for organizations operating without a crisis but under BSE conditions 92

3.5.2 Model for organization operating in first stage of crisis caused by BSE 92

3.5.3 Model for organization operating in second stage of crisis caused by BSE 94

3.5.4 Model for organization operating in third stage of crisis caused by BSE 96

3.5.5 Model for organization operating in fourth stage of crisis caused by BSE 97

3.5.6 Model for organizations, which have not survived crisis caused by BSE 99
3.6 Research results description 100

4 IT adaptability – research results 108
4.1 General remarks 108
4.2 IT adaptability positive influence on organizational performance 109
4.2.1 Organizations operating under BSE-caused conditions but not experiencing crisis 109
4.2.2 Organizations in the first stage of crisis caused by BSE 110
4.2.3 Organizations in the second stage of crisis caused by BSE 111
4.2.4 Organizations in the third stage of crisis caused by BSE 112
4.2.5 Organizations in the fourth stage of crisis caused by BSE 112
4.2.6 Organizations which have not survived the crisis caused by BSE 113
4.3 IT adaptability among organizations operating under conditions caused by BSE 114
4.3.1 EDC as an enabler of IT adaptability 115
4.4 IT adaptability boosters 116
4.4.1 Organizational attitude toward IT adaptability (institutional-level) 117
4.4.2 Employees attitude toward IT adaptability (individual-level) 118
4.4.3 IT reliability (IT-level) 119

5 Conclusions 121

Index 125

Figures

2.1 IT adaptability, job performance, organizational performance 59
2.2 IT reliability as a mediator 66
2.3 Organizational attitudes toward IT adaptability as a mediator 68
2.4 Employees' attitudes toward IT adaptability as a mediator 70
2.5 Employees' dynamic capabilities as an enabler 74
4.1 Organizations operating under BSE-caused conditions but not experiencing crisis 110
4.2 Organizations in the first stage of crisis caused by BSE 111
4.3 Organizations in the second stage of crisis caused by BSE 111
4.4 Organizations in the third stage of crisis caused by BSE 112
4.5 Organizations in the fourth stage of crisis caused by BSE 113
4.6 Organizations which have not survived the crisis caused by BSE 113

Tables

1.1	Definitions of IT	7
1.2	The COVID-19 pandemic timeline	32
1.3	Literature coverage of IT support during COVID-19	38
2.1	Dimensions of IT adaptability	57
3.1	The COVID-19 pandemic in Poland, Italy, and the USA	87
3.2	Research sample characteristic	88
3.3	Variables overview	90
3.4	Regression analysis results	91
3.5	Model overview for organizations not in crisis	92
3.6	Model effects for organizations not in crisis	93
3.7	Model overview for organizations in prodromal crisis stage	93
3.8	Model effects for organizations in prodromal crisis stage	94
3.9	Model overview for organizations in acute crisis stage	95
3.10	Model effects for organizations in acute crisis stage	95
3.11	Model overview for organizations in chronic crisis stage	96
3.12	Model effects for organizations in chronic crisis stage	97
3.13	Model overview for organizations in resolution crisis stage	98
3.14	Model effects for organizations in resolution crisis stage	98
3.15	Model overview for organizations, which did not survive crisis	99
3.16	Model effects for organizations, which did not survive crisis	100

Acknowledgments

Research was funded by National Science Center in Poland by grant No. 2020/37/B/HS4/00130 titled “Development of the Job Performance model based on Employees’ Dynamic Capabilities for various phases of crisis in organization”.

Introduction

Due to tremendous shift in the business environment of contemporary organizations (which happened due to the COVID-19 pandemic), there is a need to redefine the role and importance of information technology (IT) support, which starts to be a key for ensuring their operations and survival. The COVID-19 pandemic and restrictions which it caused started a vast transformation of the business environment, in which organizations were forced to operate and such transformation remained in place even after the main wave of the pandemic was over. Hence, from the beginning of XXI century, organizations started to operate in a much more IT-dependent world, with significantly higher dynamics and unpredictability of the environment.

It seems that organizations are slowly beginning to operate in the "day after" environment, which differs significantly from the world known from before the COVID-19 pandemic and is currently an everyday challenge for contemporary entrepreneurs, which – to make matters even worse – are still either trying to avoid a crisis or experiencing various stages of it due to turbulence of environment caused by COVID-19 itself. Moreover, much higher level of turbulence of environment and its unpredictability causes various Black Swan events (BSE) to occur more frequently than before, which may easily force those organizations into other crises.

Such new digitalized global business world and the need for IT use on a daily basis connected with the unprecedented turbulence of the environment calls for the re-analysis of paradigms known from management sciences in order to seek for new solutions enabling organizations to maintain their continuity and thrive. It was already established that after the spread of the COVID-19 pandemic, the most widely known theoretical models from management sciences were no longer appropriately explaining the behavior of organizations, which were striving to find new ways for survival under changed conditions of operating (Lee & Lee, 2021; Tønnessen et al., 2021) and it was a growing need to develop new models.

It was clear that maintaining continuity and any further development of organizations will need a significant redesign of the way of operating in such changed environment. There is already an extensive body of literature covering various positive and negative effects of the COVID-19 pandemic on

DOI: 10.4324/9781003365044-1

contemporary organizations, and some new models concerning their behavior during the pandemic are already proposed. However, researchers commonly divide their discussions into "before" and "after" the BSE or disaster (Sakurai & Murayama, 2019), which in these case means that the literature reviews concerning all the issues related to the beginning of the COVID-19 pandemic are not entirely valid for the world, which emerged due to its occurrence. Moreover, the role of IT among contemporary organizations has significantly raised and changed, and the literature coverage of that phenomena from the perspective of organizations is still very poor. Especially the holistic approach for IT use in organizations operating under such changed conditions is still not present in the literature (Pan & Zhang, 2020; Sakurai & Murayama, 2019).

It constitutes a clear research gap, showing the need to identify mechanisms, which will allow organizations operating in a new digitalized business world which emerged due to the COVID-19 pandemic to benefit from IT use. It especially concerns the use of IT under conditions of crisis caused by Black Swan events, allowing it to support organizations in avoiding crises caused by such conditions or survive them, in cases when avoiding them is not possible. Some researchers underline that it is the most current issue to identify mechanisms, which will allow to survive the BSEs, such as the COVID-19 pandemic, and prepare for the future and next BSEs causing global crises (Pan, Cui, & Qian, 2020; Pan & Zhang, 2020). It is underlined by various researchers that currently there is an important opportunity and need for scholars to "contribute to the ongoing effort is to build on the collective knowledge being created as we continue to combat the COVID-19 pandemic and respond swiftly to develop new research expertise in tackling grand challenges through responsible [IT] research" (Pan & Zhang, 2020). Those grand challenges arise especially due to the need to continue operating in the digitalized business world. It further shows that such research gap is especially important for contemporary management studies. Hence, the following research questions arise:

1. What is the role of IT in organizations operating in post-COVID-19 digitalized business world?
2. What is the mechanism of IT support for organizations avoiding crises caused by BSE?
3. What is the mechanism of IT support for organizations surviving crises caused by BSE?

It seems that from the point of view of such changed conditions, under which the organizations are forced to operate, their ability to adapt to changes may be a key for survival. The role of various dynamic capabilities for organizations operating in post-COVID-19 pandemic business environment is extensively researched recently (lit), underlining that the capability to adapt should be treated as a cornerstone for other capabilities enabling the survival of organizations. Hence, IT adaptability may have a significant role in ensuring the proper IT support and may allow organizations to gain true benefits from such support. **Therefore, the main aim of the monograph is to verify the mechanism of IT adaptability influence on organizational performance among organizations operating under conditions caused by BSE, including those which avoided a crisis caused by such conditions, those currently experiencing such crisis, and those which were not able to survive such crisis.**

The monograph will propose new theoretical model explaining the factors related to adaptable IT support and its positive influence on organizational performance of contemporary organizations. It is assumed that IT adaptability enabled by employees' dynamic capabilities influences organizational performance through organizational attitudes toward adaptable IT, employees' attitudes toward adaptable IT, IT reliability, and job performance. Such theoretical model will be empirically verified on the sample of organizations operating under the conditions of active wave of the COVID-19 pandemic in Poland, Italy, and the USA, using multigroup path analysis. Such empirically verified model will provide a basis for theory development in the field of organizational continuity and reliability during crisis caused by Black Swan event, offering the new body of knowledge related to the factors boosting organizational performance related to IT, establishing it as one of the main resources enabling organizational survival under such conditions. At the same time, it will also have utilitarian importance, as it will allow to propose conclusions and mechanisms to be used by contemporary organizations to gain more benefit from IT support and enable their higher performance under changed conditions of functioning – more IT-dependent world, with significantly higher dynamics and unpredictability of the environment.

The first chapter contains theoretical background divided into two parts. The first part concerns knowledge, theories, and models existing in the literature and defining and explaining the role of IT in organizations operating before the COVID-19 pandemic as a basis showing the growing importance of IT support, which was existing even before the shift, which was observed during the COVID-19 pandemic. The second part explains the role of Black Swan type of event in establishing new business environment: digitalized and turbulent. On the one hand, it is conducive for IT use in organization. On the other hand, organizations are forced to operate in various stages of crisis caused by such turbulent environment. Next, it shows the importance of IT support for organizations operating in it. However, the monograph concerns not only organizations operating normally (not being in crisis) but also those being in various stages of crisis. It is followed by the analysis of new needs emerging in those organizations in case of IT support showing new IT-related characteristics, which should be considered by them.

The second chapter contains the development of a new model of IT influence on organizational performance. At the beginning, IT adaptability (allowing adaptable IT support) is described as a key enabling not only organizational benefits from IT use but also organizational survival. It is followed by establishing that Black Swan type of events is a cause influencing the specific need for such IT support. Next, employees' dynamic capabilities are shown as a factor which enables the possibility of such IT support, showing the role of employees' interaction with IT. The topic is continued while describing the second part of the model, in which IT adaptability influences on organizational performance through job performance of employees and three parallel mediators on three levels of support for IT adaptability: institutional-level (organization as a whole), individual-level (employees as an element of that organization), and IT-level (IT as area of organization under the study). Based on that, the set of hypotheses is proposed, which together shape the structure of **EDC-enabled IT adaptability model of organizational performance**.

The third chapter contains description of research methodology. It presents the steps taken to perform empirical research to verify the theoretical model: questionnaire development, pilot study, and main study performed among 1,206 organizations operating in Poland, Italy, and the USA under the critical conditions of the third wave of the COVID-19 pandemic in various stages of crisis or with no crisis occurring within them or those unable to survive such crisis. Statistical reasoning based on the correlation analysis, linear regression analysis, and multigroup path analysis is presented together with the results of statistical analysis.

The fourth chapter is based on conclusions gathered during the empirical research presented in previous chapter. It shows what are the specific relations within the model among organizations operating in new digitalized and turbulent business world, under critical conditions caused by the COVID-19 pandemic as an example of BSE. The conclusions are formulated for three groups of organizations: those operating in crisis caused by such BSE, those which avoided such crisis, and those which are unable to survive such crisis. The analysis is showing the factors crucial for ensuring smooth operations of organizations in new turbulent and digitalized business world. Next, there is a specific analysis of organizations operating in each stage of crisis, determining the factors crucial for adaptable IT support in each of them, contributing to the theory of IT management and showing a different approach to the subject, which is needed among contemporary organizations.

Literature

Lee, S. M., & Lee, D. (2021). Opportunities and challenges for contactless healthcare services in the post-COVID-19 Era. *Technological Forecasting and Social Change, 167*, 120712.

Pan, S. L., & Zhang, S. (2020). From fighting COVID-19 pandemic to tackling sustainable development goals: An opportunity for responsible information systems research. *International Journal of Information Management, 55*, 102196.

Pan, S. L., Cui, M., & Qian, J. (2020). Information resource orchestration during the COVID-19 pandemic: A study of community lockdowns in China. *International journal of information management, 54*, 102143.

Sakurai, M., & Murayama, Y. (2019). Information technologies and disaster management–Benefits and issues. *Progress in Disaster Science, 2*, 100012.

Tønnessen, Ø., Dhir, A., & Flåten, B. T. (2021). Digital knowledge sharing and creative performance: Work from home during the COVID-19 pandemic. *Technological Forecasting and Social Change, 170*, 120866.

1 IT use in contemporary organizations

1.1 IT in organizations

The industrialization, which happened in the world since 18th century, is usually divided into three phases. The first phase, which started at the end of 18th century and ended at the beginning of 20th century, was based on water and steam power, and mechanical loom was one of the most significant inventions of this phase proposed in 1784. The second phase, which started at the end of 19th century and ended in early seventies of 20th century, was based on electrical energy, which made it possible to introduce the division of labor and mass production, and *assembly line* was one of the most significant inventions of this phase proposed in 1870. The third phase, which started in early seventies of 20th century and exists until the present day, was based on information technologies (IT), and *programmable logic controller (PLC)* was one of the most significant inventions of this phase proposed in 1969. Such process of industrialization made it possible to introduce the world with mechanization, electricity, and digitalization. Such world is the environment, in which contemporary organizations are operating. The mechanization and electricity are well-established and very well-utilized by those organizations, as those phases of industrialization are far behind us. However, the digitalization of organization is still at the center of attention of scholars aiming at developing theories in management sciences in the support for contemporary business world (Urbach & Rogliner, 2019).

1.1.1 IT – definition

The definition of information technology (IT) was first formulated by Whisler and Leavitt (1958). They were the pioneers of IT analysis, and in their first work, they specified that "(...) this type of technology does not yet have a single name used by everyone, so we will call them information technologies". According to Whisler and Leavitt (1958), information technologies consist of several elements that enable the processing of large amounts of information at high speed, mathematical and statistical support for organizational decisions, and intelligent thinking simulation techniques.

After the passage of time, the need arose to unify the definition of IT used by different authors. It appeared in Longley and Shain's Dictionary of

DOI: 10.4324/9781003365044-2

Professional Terminology (1985), which states that: "information technology is the acquisition, processing, storage and dissemination of sounds, images, textual and numerical information by microelectronic instruments through a combination of computing and telecommunications".

This definition has changed over the years, together with the growing potential of IT itself and their development (introduction of internet, artificial intelligence, and other developmental jumps). It is visible in several of them, according to which IT is defined as "technologies that make it possible, by intervening in the channels of information exchange, to change the course of work in an organization" (Crowston, Sawyer, & Wigand, 2001), and their main components are hardware, software, telecommunications networks, and workstations. In addition, Chan (2000) supplemented this definition stating that IT is the convergence of computer science, telecommunications, and image processing technology. Warner (2000) further added that it is also the knowledge of transforming signals from one form or medium into another. Hence, currently IT is understood as a combination of hardware, software, and communication networks (Borgmann, 2006) that enable electronic information capture, storing, processing, and transfer (Roztocki, Soja, & Weistroffer, 2019). Table 1.1 offers several different definitions of IT

Table 1.1 Definitions of IT

Definition of IT	*Source*
Those technologies engaged in the operation, collection, transport, retrieval, storage, access presentation, and transformation of information in all its forms	Boar (1997)
Technological aspect of systems of information	Hollander et al. (1999)
Creation of computer-based systems of information by using computer system in an organization	Sarosa and Zowghi (2003)
The use of automated purchasing systems, supplier links through electronic data interchange, computer-to-computer links with key suppliers, and finally systems of information	Carr and Smeltzer (2002)
All the technology that is used by an organization to collect, process, and disseminate information in all its form. Therefore, the component of information technology will include hardware (scanner, printer, computer, etc.), software (operating systems, application development language, office application, etc.)	Sarosa and Zowghi (2003)
Capabilities offered to organizations by computers, software applications, and telecommunications to deliver data, information, and knowledge to individuals and processes	Attaran (2003)
Application of information and communication technologies tools including computer network, software, and hardware required for internet connection	Tan et al. (2009)
Wide range of information processing and computer application in organizations	Onn and Sorooshian (2013)

Source: own work

currently used in the literature, showing that the level of their specificity and point of view varies extremely. However, all of them together offer a complex understanding of the notion of IT, giving the idea what should be understood by this term in the context of organization.

1.1.2 IT importance for organizations

In the last couple of years of the 20th century and the first 20 years of the 21st century, the influence of information technology (IT) has been a major topic in the management literature (Daft, 2007; Galbraith, 2014). The role of IT in organizations significantly raised because of three main factors: declining costs, improving capabilities (functions), and their increasing reliability (Cortada, 2019). It is a response to the growing need for fast and reliable access to information, which is seen by many authors as a new source of competitive advantage for organizations (e.g., Crowston, Sawyer, & Wigand, 2001; Melville, Kraemer, & Gurbaxani, 2004; Lam & Lao 2010).

The role of IT in organizations has been underlined as a factor shaping organizational performance for decades (Agarwal & Prasad, 1997). Roztocki, Soja, and Weistroffer (2019) underline that IT is crucial for socioeconomical development of modern society, which they define as "process of changes or improvements in social and economic conditions as they relate to an individual, an organization, or society as a whole". Wang (1997) at the turn of the century already established that "tremendous" number of papers were written on the topic of IT in organizations, and it was definitely not treated as one of the many various technologies available in the organization (Dewett & Jones, 2001). The literature offers insights concerning IT role in organization concerning various aspects of its functioning, including strategy (Henderson & Venkatraman, 1999; Bakos & Treacy, 1986; Croteau & Bergeron, 2001), structure (Orlikowski & Robey, 1991; Dewett & Jones, 2001), and culture (Coombs, Knights, & Willmott, 1992). Various studies confirmed that the alignment of IT with various organizational variables (like those above) makes it possible to boost organizational performance (Henderson & Venkatraman, 1999). Based on that, the main benefit for the organization from IT support is over the years most commonly connected to the improvement of performance and efficiency of processes implementation (Wang, 1997). The concept of obtaining competitive advantage based on IT use in organization emerged in the literature in previous century (Wang, 1997; Dewett & Jones, 2001), and nowadays it is clear that the functioning of the organizations is simply impossible without the support of IT. It is a well-known fact in the literature that nowadays IT disseminated to almost all processes performed by contemporary organizations (Ivanova et al., 2019). Their role is connected to both supporting the processes and automating them (Ivanova et al., 2019). According to the forecasts performer by McKinsey Global Institute before the spread of the COVID-19 pandemic, by 2036 up to 50% of work processes in the world should be automated. However, the literature covers also the issue of risks coming from implementation and use of IT in organizations (e.g. Dillon & Backhouse, 1996).

Various enablers of advantages coming from IT use in organizations are underlined in the literature. In order to present them in a systemic way, the issue of IT deployment and IT-business alignment will be discussed further.

1.1.2.1 IT deployment

The issue of IT deployment in organization, which enables a possibility to obtain those benefits from its use, connected to both organizational performance boost and competitive advantage establishment, is often discussed in the literature. There are seven main components, which enables organizations to obtain benefits from IT use. First, strategic use of IT, which allows organization to use IT in a way, which allows to gain a competitive advantage and reduce competitive disadvantages (Bergeron & Raymond, 1995). Second, management of IT, which allows to properly use current and future IT enabling its acceptance among employees and reliability, allowing for a proper use of them (Das, Zahra, & Warkentin, 1991). Third, the role of IT department, which assures the reliability of IT, plans future activities in this field and acts as a protector of IT-organization alignment (Bergeron & Raymond, 1995). Fourth, technological infrastructure, which allows to properly use IT resources and its reliability, is a key for enabling any use of IT in organization (Das Zahra, & Warkentin, 1991). Fifth, organizational infrastructure, which enables environment within organization conducive for proper IT use, ensures proper digital competences and support for the need of IT use (Henderson & Venkatraman, 1999). Sixth is administrative infrastructure, allowing the deployment of policies and actions which structures the work of employees and their use of IT (Das Zahra, & Warkentin, 1991). Seventh is technological scanning, which enables proper acquisition, analysis, and diffusion of every IT in organization (Sutcliffe, 1994). IT deployment is directly linked to organizational performance and empirical research confirms that together with business strategy is proven to enable profitability and growth of the organization (Croteau & Bergeron, 2001).

1.1.2.2 IT-business alignment

IT-business alignment emerged in the literature in the moment of focus shift concerning the way, in which organization can benefit from IT use. The researchers shifted from analyzing whether IT pays off and creates any value for organization to analyzing how such value is created (Davis, 1985; DeLone & McLean, 2003). IT-business alignment concept was introduced by Henderson and Venkatraman (1993), who proposed Strategic Alignment Model (SAM) and based on that defined it as "the degree to which the information technology mission, objectives, and plans support and are supported by the business mission, objectives, and plans" (Reich & Benbasat, 2000). The literature coverage of the issue of IT-business alignment is extremely broad and various of models and methodologies were introduced in this field over the years (e.g. Hu & Huang, 2005; Luftman, Lyytinen, & Zvi, 2017; Marchand, Kettinger, & Rollins, 2001; Reich & Benbasat, 2000). Overall, it should be stated that there are four domains of strategic alignments (Henderson & Venkatraman, 1993):

- Business strategy
- IT strategy
- Organizational infrastructure and processes
- IT infrastructure and processes

Within that, according to Luftman (1996), there are 12 alignment components: business scope, distinctive and systemic competencies, business governance, organization, infrastructure and processes, administrative structure, organization infrastructure and processes, skills, technology scope, IT governance, IT infrastructure and processes, IT infrastructure and processes architecture, IT infrastructure, and processes skills.

In his next publication (Luftman & Brier 1999), the enablers of IT-business alignment were discussed and among the most important ones, the following were included:

- senior executive support for IT,
- IT involved in strategy development,
- IT understands the business,
- business-IT partnership,
- well-prioritized IT projects,
- IT demonstrates leadership.

Among the most important inhibitors, the following were included:

- senior executives do not support IT,
- IT/business lack close relationships,
- IT does not prioritize well,
- IT fails to meet its commitments,
- IT does not understand business,
- IT management lacks leadership.

1.1.2.3 Perceived usefulness of IT support

The role of IT for contemporary organizations is also underlined by various policies and agendas of the European Union and the United Nations. Among them, two seem to be the most important: Agenda for Sustainable Development and Digital Action Plan.

Agenda for Sustainable Development underlines that IT can substantially accelerate the development progress in almost all fields, as it has the potential to greatly bridge various digital gaps occurring also in case of organization. Some authors go as far as stating that it leads the way to construct knowledge communities. Sustainable Development Goals proposed in the agenda are generally connected to "5P": People, Prosperity, Partnership, Peace, and Planet. IT is not given as a specific field, as it is visible in every "P" and its role in the achievement of each goal is undisputable. IT is treated as the key catalysts to all of the sustainable development goals and pursuing them without IT support seems impossible.

Digital Education Action Plan (2021–2027) is a new European Union policy which is connected in turn with digital competence. Digital competences are understood as the willingness and ability of "a person to confidently, efficiently, critically and safely apply information and communication technologies in various spheres of life" (Yanli & Danni, 2021).

Currently, IT adoption and further dissemination within organizations is also usually connected to the Technological Industry 4.0. Even though it seems inevitable for the contemporary world to be more and more dependent on IT and the research body connected to TI 4.0 is extremely comprehensive, it offers some distinct understanding of current enablers of growing role of IT in organizations:

- Internet (DeNardis, 2010)
- Internet of Things (Atzori, Iera, & Morabito, 2010)
- Cloud Computing (Mell & Grance, 2021)
- Fog and Mobile Cloud (Bonomi et al., 2012)
- Big Data (Chen, Mao, & Liu, 2014)
- Human-Computer Interaction (Card, Moran, & Newell, 1986)
- Artificial intelligence and robotics (Benbya, Pachidi, & Jarvenpaa, 2021)
- Open source (Feller & Fitzgerald, 2000)

However, the use of those IT enablers in organizations comes with growing number of challenges, as their support becomes more and more crucial. Aceto, Persico, and Pescapé (2019) are underlining that those challenges may be identified in groups connected to contemporary technology enablers. Among one of the most important ones, the following should be underlined:

- IT use causes challenges connected to the availability of crucial services and their performance (not only in the sense connected to network performance). Trust in the entire infrastructure is a key enabler allowing organizations to lean in and accept the long-term reality of being dependent on implemented IT (Wu, Sun, & Wolter, 2018). It also causes challenges connected with data privacy.
- Internet use (as a part of IT use) causes challenges not only with growing traffic load and need for bandwidth demands (Aceto, Persico, & Pescapé,

2019) but also with network neutrality and censorship. It also causes multiple challenges connected to all sorts of regulations, which must be obeyed.

- Human-Computer Interaction causes challenges connected to the need for rethinking it, as there is a growing need for context-sensitive user interfaces (as a part of user-centered design) (Wittenberg, 2016).

1.1.3 IT in organization – typology

There are many different types of IT used in organization. Their division, description, and characterization can be carried out due to various criteria, including:

- Elements of organization, which need IT support (distinguished on the basis of the function of the organizational unit),
- Type of user (the basis for classification is the hierarchical level to which users are assigned),
- Scope of the system (domain coverage determined by the number of organizational domain functions supported by the system, and spatial coverage distinguished on the basis of geographic or organizational coverage),
- Type of application of IT,
- Type and spatial distribution of computer hardware.

From the perspective of the presented work, it seems most relevant to present a typology of IT compiling a complete list of them. Given the accepted general definition of information technologies (information systems), their typology should be a supplement clarifying this concept. To this end, the typology of IT by the type of organizational functions they support will be described first, since it makes it possible not only to indicate the types of IT but also to clearly define the differences between them. In the second place, the typology of systems due to their domain coverage will be given, since it makes it possible to demonstrate that IT can intermingle, and in an organization, IT is most often supporting more than one type of organizational function (O'Brien & Marakas, 2012).

Typology of information systems due to the type of organizational functions supported the functions of the organization enlisted for the purpose of the division of IT into a group supporting the physical functions of the organization (Operational Support Systems OSS) and a group supporting management functions (Management Information Systems MIS) (O'Brien & Marakas, 2012).

There are three groups within **Operational Support Systems**:

- Transaction-Processing Systems (TPS), which are oriented to record the day-to-day activities of the organization, handling transactions within the organization and the organization with the environment. This group includes Sales Records Systems, Accounting Systems, Fixed Asset Management Systems, Payroll Records Systems. The first Transaction System called SABRE was introduced by American Airlines in 1960 and was capable of processing 83,000 transactions per day (Weikum & Vossen, 2001).

- Process Control Systems (PCS) – which are oriented to support all production-related tasks in an organization. There are three groups of Production Control Systems: Unit Control Systems, Batch Control Systems and Continuous Control Systems – depending on the type of manufacturing technology present in the organization.
- Enterprise Collaboration Systems (ECS) – which are oriented to support internal communication between employees due to the use of tools such as groupwear (internal conferences), Internet, Ethernet (internal network). This group includes E-mail Messaging Systems, Instant Messaging Systems, Conference Systems, and Document Sharing Systems (Ellis, Gibbs, & Rein, 1991).

There are also three groups within **Management Support Systems**.

The first of these is Management Information Systems (MIS), which are oriented toward the efficient collection, processing, and use of data in an organization through database systems. Carbonara (2005) proposed dividing Management Information Systems into three groups. Thus, she distinguished:

- Coordinating Systems – information systems that support the integration and coordination of information exchange processes occurring in the organization,
- Process Systems – information systems that support processes by converting input data into output data,
- Knowledge Management Systems – information systems that support organizational learning and problem-solving and decision-making, in addition to supporting knowledge exchange among organizational members.

The second group of Management Support Systems is Decision Support Systems, which are oriented to support strategic, tactical, and operational decision-making in an organization. They use database systems and methods oriented to support decision-making related to with partially or poorly structured problems (Tadeusiewicz, Moszner, & Szydełko, 1998).

The third group is Executive Information Systems (EIS), which operate on the basis of record-keeping and reporting systems using the organization's existing databases (Klonowski, 2004) and are oriented toward tracking the overall performance of the organization through sets of individualized queries and reports.

1.1.4 IT life cycle

According to Stewart (2008), a prerequisite for a complete description of IT in an organization is to determine what stage of the life cycle it is in. The concept of the technology life cycle has its roots in the science of technology management. Technology management (TM – Technology Management) is a process that includes planning, directing, controlling, and coordinating the development and implementation of technological capabilities (Cetindamar, Phaal, & Probert, 2009). It is increasingly being defined that technology management refers to the exploitation and improvement of time-varying technological capabilities (Best, 2001). According to Jin and Zedtwitz (2008), IT management enables the effective use of technical knowledge and skills – not only to improve and develop products and processes but also to improve existing IT and create new knowledge and skills in response to increased competitiveness in the market. However, to meet this, it is necessary to synchronize technology development with the current requirements of the organization. This synchronization is described by the technology life cycle. It is also one of the techniques of strategic analysis to diagnose the degree of technology development, which is necessary when developing, operating, or introducing new technologies (Gierszewska & Romanowska 2003).

Many different versions of the technology life cycle can be found in the literature, most often consisting of four to six stages:

- Cetindamar, Phaal, and Probert (2009): identification, selection, acquisition, implementation and exploitation, protection, learning
- Gregory (1995): identification, selection acquisition, exploitation, protection
- Rush, Bessant, and Hobday (2007): search, selection strategy, acquisition, skill acquisition, implementation and exploitation, learning
- Sumanth (1997): awareness of need, acquisition and refinement, adaptation
- Dogson (2000): selection strategy, collaboration, research and development, commercialization
- Cotec (1998): scanning, selection, implementation, learning
- Levin and Bernard (2008): knowledge creation, requirements analysis, organizational support

However, it is worth noting that the listed cycles are universal and do not apply only to information technologies. Despite the differences in names, the subsequent stages remain the same in many cases. For example, the commercialization stage (indicated by Dogson (2000)) consists of the same set of activities as the exploitation stage (indicated by Gregory (1995)). Cetindamar, Phaal, and Probert (2009), on the other hand, understand the exploitation stage as a different, limited set of activities, and only after supplementing it with activities related to implementation, it will correspond to the exploitation stage indicated by Gregory (1995). It seems that the technology life cycle presented by Cetindamar, Phaal, and Probert (2009) is the most complete. The authors point out that this cycle is particularly applicable in the field of information technology. After a careful analysis of the list of activities developed by various authors that make up the various stages of the life cycle, it can be concluded that, in fact, the model proposed by Cetindamar, Phaal, and Probert (2009) is most applicable to the specifics of information technology.

However, it seems necessary to make an adjustment in the proposed set of activities. This set of technology implementation activities should be clearly assigned to the acquisition stage. Between the acquisition stage and the exploitation stage, there must be a point at which the technologies are physically introduced into the organization – this is the closing point of the acquisition stage. This is because it highlights the fundamental difference that exists between the activities of implementation (introducing information technologies into the organization) and exploitation (using them in the organization). In addition, the preservation and learning stages are complementary by reference to the period in which the organization learns lessons from all previous stages.

Therefore, the IT life cycle should contain five stages: identification, selection, acquisition and implementation, exploitation, and protection and learning.

The IT identification stage focuses on the identification of an organization's technology needs, which is carried out in the context of the organization's business processes and with the participation of employees with a direct interest in the studied area of its operation. Identification is not limited to assessing the needs for IT alone, as market conditions are also taken into account. As part of identification, a solution is sought, an audit is conducted, data is collected, and solutions are analyzed and evaluated.

The IT selection stage requires the involvement of employees from different business units. It is a decision-making process that takes into account the relevant strategic goals of the organization, which requires an effective assessment and qualification of the organization's particular needs. Selection should begin by identifying all constraints and priorities arising from the organization's strategy. These are then related to the capabilities of individual IT, selecting the necessary functions.

The IT acquisition and implementation stage first consists of acquiring the selected IT based on a decision related to the choice made according to "develop technologies – develop technologies in cooperation with a third party – buy technologies" (Cetindamar, Phaal, & Probert, 2009). Indeed, the development of technologies can take place through the use of knowledge and skills possessed by employees or by outsiders. In the second place, activities related to the implementation of technology are carried out, i.e., with the implementation of acquired technologies into the organization. Thus, there is a transfer of technology from the R&D department or from their manufacturer and their deployment in the organization.

The stage of IT exploitation is aimed at either generating profit or achieving other goals set to be achieved at the time of technology selection. Exploitation consists of, among other things, secondary implementation, amendment process, and marketing.

The IT preservation and learning stage is primarily the protection of acquired knowledge and experience supporting the existence of IT in the organization. It concerns archiving materials, formalization of procedures, and such processes as patenting or applying for protection of intellectual value. Learning and drawing lessons learned at all previous stages of the IT life cycle is an essential link in it, and activities related to the protection and learning stage are critical to the proper management of information technology in an organization, as they enable the improvement of future processes related to the technology life cycle.

When analyzing information technology in an organization, it is important to identify the stage of its life cycle. This will bring some order to the considerations and provide the right point of view – for example, the degree of dissemination or acceptance of a technology may be analyzed only at the stage of technology exploitation and analyzing it at earlier stages may lead to erroneous conclusions.

1.1.5 IT adoption models and IT success models

The one universally accepted effective approach the understanding of IT adoption in organizations, which is directly connected to the increase of employees' (acting as users) acceptance and their subsequent use of IT has still not emerged in the literature (Kukafka et al., 2003). Therefore, it seems to be a fundamental challenge of management sciences in the fields of IT use in organizations to offer a solution enabling organizations to gain as much benefit from IT use as possible. Over the years, various models for achieving such aim were developed.

First model, which emerged in the literature, was called Diffusion of Innovations Model (DOI) in 1962 and was developed by Rogers (Miller, 2015). It showed that diffusion is a process in which certain channels are used to communicate innovations (connected with IT) among members of organization. It is developed around the concept of relative advantage, which is understood as the degree to which the invention is perceived to be better than what it supersedes.

Next, Social Construction of Technology Model (SCOT) emerged in 1984 and was developed by Pinch and Bijaker (Pinch, 2012). It showed that technology and its use is directly shaped by human actions. With the introduction of this model, the authors postulated that technology constructivism should replace technology determinism.

Next, the most widely known Technology Acceptance Model (TAM) emerged in 1985, which was developed by Davis (1985). The model introduced the perspective of employees and their willingness to use the technology.

Next, in 1990, two different models emerged. One of them was developed by DeSanctis and Poole (1994) – it is called Adaptive Structuration Theory (AST). The model assumes that employees (organizational actors) are crucial in affecting outcomes of the organization (including those connected with IT) and they are able to intentionally adapt rules and resources in order to achieve those outcomes (organizational goals). The other one was developed by DePietro, Wiarda and Fleischer (1990) – it is called Technology-Organization-Environment Framework (TOE). This model underlines that technology innovations and decision-making connected to them are influenced by technological context, organizational context and environmental context.

Next, Task-Technology Fit model (T-T Fit) emerged in 1995 and was developed by Goodhue and Thompson (1995). The main idea behind the model is that IT should by well-fitted with the tasks, which it is supposed to support and its actual use is crucial for its adoption in organization.

Next, in 1995, Technology Affordance Theory (TAT) was introduced by Hutchby (1995). The model underlines that the benefits coming from the use of IT are not only connected to the products of users' work but mainly to the accomplishments of the entire organizational system using IT (interface between employee's tasks and technology affordance). The concept of technology affordance is connected to the possibilities of technology itself, not only capabilities of its users. Such perspective broadened the understanding of IT adoption, underlining that organization should emphasize the need for maximize the benefits obtained from used IT, enabling employees to use it in every possible way.

Finally, the Unified theory of acceptance and use of technology (UTAUT) emerged in 2003 and until today it is another one of the most known and widely used model connected to IT adoption. It was developed by Venkatesh et al. (2003) and is offering a perspective broadening the understanding shown in TAM model.

1.1.5.1 TAM model

The acceptance of IT seems to still be at the center of attention of scholars, who want to underpin the factors influencing organization's ability to benefit from the IT. Therefore, it seems crucial to understand the idea behind the concept of technology acceptance. The basis for the analysis of technology acceptance was the methods for surveying user satisfaction (members of an organization using technology to perform tasks) developed by Bailey and Pearson (1983). They identified 39 factors that could affect user satisfaction resulting from the use of technology and thus the level of technology acceptance. Since such a long list of factors was not practical, attempts were made to modify it. Cheney, Mann, and Amoroso (1986) grouped them into three categories: uncontrollable, partially controllable, and fully controllable, still focusing only on the level of user satisfaction.

Davis (1985) conducted a series of scientific studies devoted to assessing technology acceptance in an organization and introduced Technology Acceptance Model (TAM), which made it possible to determine the degree of technology acceptance in an organization and to estimate the actual degree of technology use in an organization on this basis. Davis (1985) continued Bailey and Pearson's (1983) research on measuring user satisfaction, motivated by a desire to determine which factors influence whether users will adopt or reject a new technology. The TAM model presents a mechanism for the influence of external factors (including the characteristics of the technology implemented in an organization and its availability, which will be described in detail later in the chapter) on internal factors (such as employees' beliefs, intentions, or beliefs).

The two main factors introduced in the TAM model that make up the actual degree of technology use in an organization are: the anticipated usefulness of the technology and the ease of use of the technology.

It is through these that external factors influence internal factors. Anticipated usefulness is defined as the degree to which a person believes that using a particular system will increase the efficiency of the work he or she does (Moore & Benbasat, 1991). This definition is rooted in the understanding of the word useful: one that is capable of being used for the benefit of the user. This is relevant in the context of the fact that in organizations employees are sometimes rewarded for the efficiency of their work. Thus, technology is considered useful if the user believes there is a positive correlation between using it and the effectiveness of the work performed. Expected ease of use is defined as the degree to which a person believes that using a particular system will not require excessive effort (Moore & Benbasat, 1991). This definition, in turn, is rooted in the understanding of the word ease – the absence of difficulty or effort. Effort is the value one can expend on the various tasks one is responsible for performing. Thus, technology is easy to use if the user believes that accomplishing tasks with it will be easier than accomplishing them without it.

These two factors influence the willingness to use technology and the behavioral intentions of members of an organization to use it which in turn translates into the actual degree of technology use in the organization.

The degree of acceptance of IT will therefore show the actual degree of its use by organizational members. Dillon (2001, p. 1105) defines it as the apparent willingness of a group of users to use information technology while performing the tasks it was designed to support.

However, from the point of view of organization, lack of acceptance is potentially most devastating and may cause lack of benefits coming from IT use. Lack of acceptance is often caused by reasons related to the low anticipated usefulness of the technology (employees believe that it is not essential to their work) or the high difficulty of use (e.g., because its operation is unclear). With the increase in the spread of IT accompanied by a lack of acceptance, the following two scenarios can be considered:

- Although employees have access to IT, they perform their tasks in the existing way, because they believe that this is a more efficient choice. IT in this case in the organization exists but has no real impact on the rest of the organization due to its non-use.
- Employees are forced by external factors to use an unaccepted IT, which leads to inappropriate and incomplete use of the IT, and therefore their impact on other elements of the organization is incomplete.

In both of these cases, studying the relationship between IT and any other elements of the organization is impossible due to the fact that their use in the organization would be apparent – the IT implemented in the organization would not support the functions for which they were intended.

1.1.5.2 PRECEDE model

The development of the approaches, which allow organizations to understand the ways, in which they can boost their benefits coming from IT use was also connected to building on models concerning different notions, such as PRECEDE. PRECEDE is a conceptual framework of two components used extensively as the basis for planning health promotion programs and was developed by Green and Kreuter (1999). Based on it, Kukafka et al. (2003) proposed a model, which they called IT implementation framework. The model assumes that there are five elements connected to the existence of IT in organization, determining the level of benefits which may be obtained by organization which uses it:

- organizational needs and goals, allowing to choose a proper IT and identifying its value for all stakeholders,
- *organizational needs amenable to IT system solutions*, allowing to identify all system specifications and their importance for stakeholders,
- *behaviors linked with system use, allowing to identify the behaviors of employees connected with the use of proposed IT, noting various environmental factors (physical, social) which may influence those behaviors,*
- *factors associated with behaviors, allowing to identify factors influencing behaviors of employees connected to the use of IT, providing context for their motivation and introduction of reinforcement factors,*
- *system use-inducing strategies, allowing to develop and implement systemic approaches conducive for proper use of IT.*

1.1.5.3 IT success model

The IT success model was developed by DeLone and McLean (2003) and to this day is one of the most recognized and comprehensive ones. The first version was published by the authors in 1992. This model indicated that the success of IT solutions in the organization is caused by the positive impact of IT on the entire organization, which has its source in the positive IT impact on individual employees. The impact of IT on users is, according to the authors, dependent on the actual use of it during everyday work, and this in turn is conditioned by the quality of the system itself and the information contained in it. The entire idea behind the DeLone and McLean (2003) approach lies in the development of the process model, showing the cause-effect relations between elements and causality flows.

The first empirically verified model of IT success introduced two elements: the quality of system and the quality of information, which translate into use and user satisfaction and further, into individual impact and organizational impact. Such model clearly confirms that benefits obtained by organization through IT support are enabled by employees, who actually use those technologies (DeLone & McLean, 2003). The authors published ten years update of the initial model, offering some changes based on the literature review of their idea. The corrected model of IT success introduces three elements: the quality of the system and the quality of information contained in it and the quality of the support service of this system, which influences intention to use the IT (and next, its actual use) and user satisfaction, which translated into net benefits. The new independent variable – the quality of support services – was introduced by Pitt et al. (1995) with some troubles (the authors mixed the properties of IT itself with the properties of IT department). However, even with those shortcomings, the authors decided to include it in the amended model.

Various authors started a debate concerning the idea behind the name of the model, stating that it should reflect the use of IT, not its success. Seddon (1997) offered the new version of the name and spoke about IT success and use model. It was one of the many approaches offering amended and changed models, which were derived from the initial DeLone and McLean (2003) model.

1.1.6 The need for a new model for IT use

Although there are many models connected to IT adoption and use, they are all widely criticized in the literature and the arguments are usually the same, not depending on the type of the model. Xu and Lu (2022) are stating that regardless of their extensive use, TAMs and UTAUTs are "widely questioned and criticized by their suitability, sufficiency, and robust for explaining and predicting technology use, especially in workplace settings where IT system use may be mandatory instead of voluntary". It should be underlined that even though they are usually treated as equal in the literature, there is a big difference between TAM and UTAUT. TAM is designed for voluntary use of IT and UTAUT is designed for mandatory use of such. It seems that those to approaches needed some complex approach. However, there are many similar weak aspects of those models, but four of three are most discussed (Ajibade, 2018; Malatji, Eck, & Zuva, 2020; Xu & Lu, 2022): the link between intention and actual use is not properly developed, as the intention of use may not always translate into actual use, the behavior cannot be fully determined just by perceived usefulness and perceived ease of use, perceived ease of use cannot be treated as a stable variable and a lot of various factors influences it. However, what is even more important, various authors underline that self-reported use data are not valid to assess any aspects of IT use in organizations and the perspective of managers and their view of entire organization should be included (Ajibade, 2018; Malatji, Eck, & Zuva, 2020). Moreover, Bagozzi (2007) stated that TAM and UTAUT do not allow to recognize the effect of the group and consider individual users only. In case of contemporary organizations, it seems to be lacking an important point of view because of that.

There are also concerns connected to IT success models. Over the years, vast number of articles were published on the topic of the DeLone and McLean (2003) model verification and amendments. Among various propositions, there were those connected to user involvement and top management support (DeLone & McLean, 2003). It remains in line with a view of Lyytinen and Hirschheim (1987), who stated earlier that any IT that is not used (abandoned by users) should be considered to have an interaction failure and user involvement is crucial for mitigating such risk. Even though authors recognize the need for including such point of view, it was never offered in the amended models by the authors. Seddon (1997) verified such amendment and his empirical research confirmed that user involvement is indeed significantly, but not directly, influencing elements of the model. However, in the context of the IT success model, such views were further developed showing the need for separating the intention to use from actual use of IT. Intention to use is an attitude of employees, which may be influences by various factors and is crucial enabler of any benefits, which can be obtained by organization from IT support. Petter, DeLone, and McLean (2008) performed a meta-analysis of studies connected to the IT success model verification and analyzed variables within the model from the individual level point of view. They confirmed the importance of actual use and strongly suggested that it is influenced by intention of use, without which actual use will not happen. Such findings are confirmed by Turner et al. (2010), who verified that intention of use is indeed a strong predictor of actual use, but those are separate concepts.

Moreover, Mardiana, Tjakraatmadja, and Aprianingsih (2015) suggest that IT adoption models should not be treated as a separate approach for the analysis of IT in organization, as they are somehow included in the idea of DeLone and McLean (2003) success model. It is strongly suggested that IT acceptance (offered in TAM or UTAUT) has the potential to shape such intention of use, underlining to greater extent the need to include the employees' perspective while considering the factors shaping IT success in organization. Such findings were confirmed by various authors, including Yousafzai, Foxall, and Pallister (2007), who verified the relation between TAM and actual use of IT. It also allows to put into the model the concept of performance expectations (one of the variables in UTAUT model allows to measure how – according to the user – the use of IT influences job performance) (Chan et al., 2010).

Therefore, it seems that there is a need for new approach to the analysis of benefits, which may be obtained by organization due to IT use, which includes all those suggestions, which were present in the literature even before the fast digitalization process started due to the COVID-19 pandemic. It should stay in line with views presented by Seddon (1997), who underlined that the model describing IT use in organization in any manner should focus on benefits obtained through various factors (like use, user satisfaction, etc.), not those individual factors alone. The rapidly changing business world and new reality, in which contemporary organizations operate additionally underline such need, as the approach and understanding of the importance of IT use in organizations changed tremendously and the role of employee, as a user, have also risen to the level of an enabler and guardian of proper IT use.

1.2 Crisis as a cause for change of the perspective on IT

Crisis is commonly defined in the literature as "a low-probability, high-impact situation that is perceived by critical stakeholders to threaten the viability of the organization" (Pearson & Clair, 1998). Various other authors are proposing other characteristics, which are added to this definition, like: rarity, significance, impact level, viability threatening (James, Wooten, & Dushek, 2011; Williams et al., 2017). Hermann (1963) was one of the first scholars, who approached the subject of crisis within the organization. Among other things, he indicated that there are three key components of an organizational crisis: (1) it creates a threat to at least some high-priority values of the organization, (2) it creates a short window of time for a response, and (3) it is usually unexpected or unanticipated by the organization.

There are two main perspectives in research concerning crisis in the current literature: crisis-as-event and crisis-as-process.

The crisis-as-event perspective understands crisis as a "low-probability, unanticipated, high impact (i.e., harmful) events that are unpredictable, surprising, and threaten the viability of the organization" (Lagadec, 2007; Pearson & Clair, 1998). In this perspective, a distinct event is a main focus of the analysis as a source of crisis. Such perspective caused many crises typology to arise, as it indicates that there is a clear and well-defined cause of crisis, which does not need further investigation to clarify it. The crisis-as-process perspective understands crisis as "processes extended in space and time, where a "triggering event" is the result of a long period of incubation; that is, crises occur in phases" (Roux-Dufort, 2007, 2016; Shrivastava, 1995; Turner, 1976). In this perspective, crisis is developed through a long process, which allows to detect numerous warning signals based on which its occurrence may be somehow predicted (as an isolated event or a sum of problems adding into each other) (Williams et al., 2017).

However, authors connected to both of those approaches, related to both societal or organizational crisis, are underlining that every crisis is "characterized by non-trivial threats to life, well-being, or other significantly held values, by unpredictability, and by urgency" (Falkheimer & Heide, 2006). That is why the issue of avoiding and overcoming potential crisis should be at the center of every contemporary organization.

1.2.1 Crisis typologies

Over the years, several various typologies of crisis emerged in the literature (Gundel, 2005), which concern various points of view. Gundel (2005) stated that there are two main concepts, on which modern typologies are based: distinguishing crises based on main cause of them of distinguishing crises based on their main traits.

The most typologies have a general overtone. One of the most commonly used and oldest typologies distinguishes between man-made (technological) and natural causation (e.g. 't Hart, Rosenthal, & Kouzmin, 1993). It has various types, including a newer version which offer three groups: man-made, natural, and social crises (e.g. Rike, 2003).

However, there are also more specific typologies. They usually depict a wide range of possible groups, like e.g. mine disasters, oil spills, air disasters, crowd disasters, nuclear crises, terrorism, or chemical explosions ('t Hart, Rosenthal, & Kouzmin, 1993).

Moreover, usually after a world-altering event (for example such as 9/11 terrorist attack), some new typologies arise based on the assumption that previous ones are outdated as they have not offered a specific place for such an event. Mitroff and Alpaslan (2003) proposed a new typology adding a third group into two groups usually offered in previous literature studies, which included intentional or abnormal accidents (like bombings or kidnappings), besides normal accidents (like system-overloads) and natural disasters.

However, there are also typologies which are based on one selected trait/characteristic of crisis, for example: national or international crises, episodic or continuous crisis management, and corporate or public crises ('t Hart, Rosenthal, & Kouzmin, 1993; 't Hart, Heyse, & Boin, 2001). It should be stated that they are usually not widely used as they are often developed for the purpose of a specific study, which needs to distinguish crises based on a specific characteristic.

The typologies, which have a more general nature, allow to form overall conclusions and research the issue on more general and abstract level, which allows to the analysis of all characteristics and traits, which various crisis grouped in one widely spread type has in common. However, it does not allow for the distinction between crises within such wide group, which are definitely characterized by various more specific traits, which distinguish one from the other.

The ťypologies, which have less general nature and more specific groups of crises, allow to analyze each of them more precisely, practically guaranteeing that the crises placed in one group will have most traits in common and may be researched as homogenous group. However, it is easy to propose the typology in which the number of groups of crises is simply too high for it to be useful to be a basis for some overall conclusions.

One of the typologies, which takes from the advantages of both approaches, was offered by Gundel (2005), who stated that there are two most important characteristics of crisis: predictability and influence possibility. He stated that crisis is predictable, "if place, time or in particular the manner of its occurrence are knowable to at least a third competent party and the probability of occurrence is not to be neglected". He also stated that crisis "can be influenced if responses to stem the tide or to reduce damages by antagonizing the causes of a crisis are known and possible to execute". It should be stated that crises, which can be directly influenced, are the only ones which respond in any ways to crisis management and can be mitigated with mechanisms occurring within the organization. Therefore, when the influence possibility is high, such mechanisms are possible, usually well-known, and should allow to significantly change the situation within the organization, influencing its ability to survive the crisis. Based on those two characteristics, Gundel (2005) proposed a matrix typology of crises, distinguishing four types: conventional crises, unexpected crises, intractable crises, and fundamental crises.

1.2.1.1 Conventional crisis: predictable, sensitive to influence, with well-known influence possibilities

This type of crisis concerns mainly disasters of technological systems. Examples are ferry disasters and plant explosions.

Those crises are usually well-defined, various countermeasures may be developed before their occurrence and it is not a challenge to plan for them. Specific crisis can of course be characterized by some specific traits, but usually it is possible to form overall conclusions and offer overall countermeasures and plans for preparation for such crises. Organizations can use an integrated system quality standards and include basics of crisis management (Pun & Hui, 2002). They also have various regulatory policies created outside of the organization in place to help them respond to such crises.

1.2.1.2 Unexpected crisis: unpredictable, sensitive to influence

This type of crisis also concerns mainly technological systems, however with some non-standard attributes or situations which occur infrequently caused by natural systems. An example is Tunnel blaze in Austria in 2000, when non-flammable funicular railway burnt down.

Those crises are impossible to predict but after their occurrence, there is a well-known set of measures which can be deployed in order to countermeasure the negative effects of the crisis. However, it is impossible to implement any prevention measures, as it is not possible to predict the crisis. There are known ways for fighting such unexpected events within organizations, which are connected to the employment of qualified employees, developing think-thanks within the organization or implementing better-quality technology.

1.2.1.3 Intractable crisis: predictable, not sensitive to influence

This type of crisis concerns technological, natural, or social systems, which are characterized by the high possibility of disaster or problem occurring, which is connected to other characteristics making it impossible to correctly influence it. Technological example is the Chernobyl incident. Social example is the UEFA-Cap final in 1985 between Italy and Grate Britain, where 39 people died. Natural example is earthquakes.

Those crises, due to their lack of sensitivity for influence, are characterized by difficulties in preparing for their occurrence, even though they can be easily predicted. Such crises are usually connected with various conflicts of interest which surrounds them and makes it impossible to implement any proactive countermeasures. It is usually a well-known fact that the danger exists, but it is not possible to prevent them or prepare for them. Organizations may foster a safety culture as a countermeasure, promoting anticipation of such disasters. However, usually more than one organization if affected by this type of crisis and organization itself cannot efficiently fight the negative effects, as overall policies and regulations are needed.

1.2.1.4 Fundamental crisis: unpredictable, not sensitive to influence

This type of crisis concerns inexplicable natural, technological, and social disasters. Examples are 9/11 terrorist attack and the COVID-19 pandemic.

Such crises are characterized by their lack of possibility to be predicted and lack of available mechanisms to influence them when they occur. It is not possible to prepare for such crisis, as it is usually appearing unpredictably and any responses which can be taken are unknown in the moment of crisis occurrence (or those which are known are not sufficient). That is why it is the most dangerous type of crisis, with the potential to do the most damage to organizations and highest level of potential destruction. There are no general recommendation or policies which may help organizations avoid such type of crisis or prepare for fighting it before it happens. One of the only few available countermeasures is establishing think-thanks, as groups of experts who will analyze all possible scenarios and look for possible crises, developing countermeasures for them.

1.2.2 BSE as a specific type of crisis

The research on Black Swan Events (BSE) started long before the term "Black Swan" was proposed formally by Taleb (2005) in the book called "The Black Swan. The Impact of the Highly Improbable". As per Taleb (2005), "A Black Swan is a highly improbable event with three principal characteristics; it is unpredictable, it carries a massive impact, and after the fact, we concoct an explanation that makes it appear less random, and more predictable than it was". The research concerning BSE is available in almost all areas of management literature (Parameswar, Chaubey, & Dhir, 2021), even though the starting point was connected to the financial management (Accomazzo & Rivadeneyra, 2009; Dohale et al., 2020).

Nowadays, three distinct categories of BSE can be identified (Flage & Aven, 2015): unknown unknowns, unknown knowns, and events with negligible probability. Donald Rumsfeld, who was at that time the United States Secretary of Defense, added one more group and restated at a press briefing on 12 February 2002 that there should be four categories of BSE: unknown unknowns, unknown knowns, known unknown, and known knowns. However, it is not a scientific-based approach and it offers a complex viewpoint of BSE, which is happening in the contemporary world.

There is a solid body of research indicating the need for organizations to develop various adequate skills, which allow them to survive BSE and they are usually connected to the ability to scan the environment and increase their preparedness for BSE occurrence (Higgins, 2014; Wardman & Mythen, 2016).

1.2.2.1 Crisis caused by BSE – research perspective

While considering the crisis from the point of view of BSE as a source, the crisis-as-event approach prevails. As stated by Roux-Dufort (2007), the crisis-as-event perspective focuses mainly on the aftermath of the event itself (which caused a crisis), while the crisis-as-process perspective focuses on the analysis of the sources of crisis and crisis-fostering environment. In such a case, as stated before, crises are seen as unanticipated contingent event (as opposed to routines and long-term processes) which is defined and isolated in space and time, and has a clear and well-defined source or cause, characterized by a high impact of it (Pearson & Clair, 1998; Shrivastava, 1995; Weick, 1988; Williams et al., 2017). Such definition fits very well with crises, which are caused by BSE – events, which are well-defined, can be established as a clear source of crisis, however as they are usually impossible to anticipate and while they are happening, the organizations are striving to survive and contain the crisis. The possibility for the extended analysis of pre-crisis environment and detailed investigation of its cause is not needed in this case. The crisis-as-process perspective aims at understanding that there is a "genealogy of crises that may be potentially tracked long before the acute phase"

(Roux-Dufort, 2016) is not only not needed, but first of all – impossible – in case of BSE.

Hence, it confirms that the crisis-as-event perspective which by definition fosters research focused on organizations' reaction to crisis caused by such rare and exceptional events (Williams et al., 2017), neglecting the issue of understanding why the crisis happened in the organization (Roux-Dufort, 2016; Weick, Sutcliffe, & Obstfeld, 1999) is more suitable here.

Moreover, the crisis-as-event perspective is usually linked in the literature with lack of the possibility to fully plan for such triggering event to occur and measure the probability of its occurrence (Pearson & Clair, 1998), which determined that any measures taken to overcome such crisis should be aimed at managing conditions, which are uncertainty-inconceivable, unstructured, unplanned, unexpected, and have high levels of dynamics (Rosenthal, 2003; Topper & Lagadec, 2013; Williams et al., 2017). Therefore, once again such perspective is suitable for crises that are caused by BSE.

However, focusing only on crisis-as-event perspective in case of BSE is not an approach, which allows to fully investigate the situation and therefore, such perspective alone may not be enough to propose valid mechanisms for organizations, which are experiencing crises caused by BSE. The crisis-as-event perspective should be supplemented by some elements of crisis-as-process perspective, connected to the analysis of stages of occurring crisis. Of course, it will be not possible to adopt a model, which characterizes by a broad set of pre-crisis stages aiming at determining the possibility of crisis occurrence and sources of it. Nevertheless, most of the known and widely used models are indicating only one stage before the crisis begins in the organization, linked to the signals, which may be detected in order to determine that crisis may happen within the organization. Such perspective is also valid for BSE as a source of crisis as it should be clearly indicated that the occurrence of BSE is a source of crisis and there is a time delay between BSE occurrence and the starting point of crisis within the organization. Moreover, organizations, which are quicker to properly detect and understand that BSE, which occurred has the potential to cause such crisis, are more prone to avoid it or survive it more efficiently (because of having more time to prepare). Therefore, even though BSE as a source of crisis should trigger the analysis to be based on crisis-as-event perspective, the elements of crisis-as-process are still valid and should be used. Such a mixed perspective will be assumed in this study, adopting one of the crisis management models, which is more suitable for such a mixed perspective.

The research concerning any BSE is in general divided into three perspectives: Pre-Black Swan event stage, Black Swan event stage, and post-Black Swan event stage (Parameswar, Chaubey, & Dhir, 2021). The meta-analysis of research concerning various BSE conducted by showed that those three perspectives offer different insights concerning changes caused by such BSE. Pre-Black Swan event research is focused on the analysis of BSE history, prediction of BSEs, and preparedness for next BSEs based on the historical information available. It also connects with identifying triggers for BSEs, allowing to predict them to some extent (as by definition it is not possible to fully predict their occurrence). Black Swan event stage research is connected to the analysis of their types and ways of managing through the critical conditions, which they are causing. Post-Black Swan event stage is organized around various short-term and long-term consequences of those events, which are usually divided into four groups: effects on organizations, effects on economy/industries, effects of specific countries, and effects of entire world. From the perspective of characterizing the new business environment, which arose after the BSE, the third stage research are the most important ones, as they are trying to present the new characteristics, which will create an environment in which organizations will operate for the following years. Therefore, the analysis of crisis caused by BSE, including crisis-as-event and crisis-as-process perspectives, should take into account those three points of view as well, which further underlines the need for mixing those two perspectives, in place of sole use of crisis-as-event one.

1.2.2.2 Crisis caused by BSE – stages

Scholars underline that there are three main approaches to crisis analysis within the organization, which got the most literature coverage over the years (Boudreaux, 2005). There are a basic three-stage model, Fink's (1986) four-stage model, and Mitroff's (1994) five-stage model.

The three-stage model has not had one specific scholar or a group of scholars, which are connected to its development (Boudreaux, 2005). It emerged in the literature as the first element connected to the development of the theory of crisis management and became a general analytical framework (Seeger et al., 2003). Coombs (1999) indicates that there are three basic stages: pre-crisis, crisis, and post-crisis and they can be treated as a macrostage, used as a basis for more particular models to be developed. The pre-crisis is connected to crisis prevention and proactive planning. The crisis is connected to crisis recognition and countermeasures development (redesign, reconfiguration of resources). The post-crisis is connected to realignment to normal functioning.

The four-stage model by Fink (1986) assumes the following stages (Boudreaux, 2005):

Prodromal stage (when the event, which will cause the crisis already happened, but the full-blown crisis has not started yet).

This stage is connected with preparedness and mitigation. It occurs before the full-blown crisis is starting within the organization and is usually treated as preparatory stage. At this stage, organization should be focused on monitoring the environment for any potential threats, mainly those connected to the BSE which happened. Moreover, the analysis of conditions under which organization will be operating due to BSE happening should be performed, potential crises overview should take place, together with the development of potential countermeasures for them. In this stage, the crisis management plan should be developed together with the plan for crisis communication.

From the perspective of BSE, it is an important stage, as it is the one in which the time delay between BSE and crisis starting point is happening. It means that during this time, the organization has the ability to detect the possibility that crisis may happen and develop and implement countermeasures, which will allow the organization to quickly resolve the crisis, if it will be impossible to avoid it.

1.2.2.2.1 ACUTE CRISIS STAGE (WHEN THERE IS SUDDEN ONSET OF CHANGES, MOST TURBULENT, AND UNPREDICTABLE)

In this stage, the crisis in organization is happening and resulting damage is becoming visible. The depth and severity of crisis will depend on the way in which organization behaved during the previous stage of crisis. Quick and proactive identification of potential crisis based on the analysis of BSE has the potential to reduce negative effects, which the crisis will have on organization. This stage is connected with assessing, activating, and alerting. After the identification of the nature of the crisis occurring within the organization, it is crucial to alert the community about it and activate existing resources and plans.

1.2.2.2.2 CHRONIC CRISIS STAGE (WHEN ORGANIZATION IS TRYING TO RESPOND TO CRISIS, WHICH IS STILL HAPPENING)

It refers to all lasting effects of crisis. Even though the BSE may have a short- or long-term character, even when BSE itself is already finished, the lasting effects of crisis which it caused within the organization will be in place for long. This stage is connected with taking actions. During this stage, the organization is experiencing full range of positive and negative effects of crisis, which is occurring and based on the previous stage, it should be equipped and ready to take actions to countermeasure the crisis and contain it.

1.2.2.2.3 RESOLUTION STAGE (WHEN THE ORGANIZATION IS RETURNING TO PRE-CRISIS FUNCTIONING)

In this stage, the definite end of crisis occurs. Its occurrence depends on actions taken by the organization in previous stages of crisis and is usually considered as a goal of the organization aiming at surviving the crisis. This stage is connected with recovering. It is the time to assess the damage, which was done within the organization due to the crisis and follow through the recovery plan to fully realign the organization with changed conditions of the environment, redesigning the organization and reconfiguring the resources for the "new normal", in which to organization will operate from now on.

Moreover, this stage is also connected to the ability of organization to learn from the crisis, which occurred. In case of BSE, it also means to establish new crisis management plans, which are more suitable in case of incidents, which cannot be predicted, including all good practices, which came from the crisis which is currently ending. It is what distinguishes the five-stage model developed by Mitroff (1994), who added additional stage at the end of his model connected to such activities: learning.

For the purpose of this study, the Fink (1986) four-stage model of crisis will be adopted, as it seems that it is most suitable for crisis caused by BSE, allowing the time delay between BSE occurrence and crisis starting point to be indicated in one of the stages. It is also showing that there is a need for distinguishing the stage in which organizations are developing countermeasures (as they are not already in place, which is in line with the character of BSE) and in which organizations are implementing them in order to contain the crisis, underlining to importance of efficient development and implementation. Moreover, it shows the clear moment of crisis ending, when the response of the organization to the BSE can be fully assessed.

1.2.2.3 Crisis management in various crisis stage

Stages of crisis emerged in the literature as a lens, through which crisis management is occurring. Crisis management is presented by Williams et al. (2017) as set of activities aimed at restoring the equilibrium in the organization and is usually defined as "individual and organizational readjustment of basic assumptions, as well as behavioral and emotional responses aimed at recovery and readjustment" (Pearson & Clair, 1998). Therefore, it should be stated that the main aim of the crisis management is to maintain the continuity of functioning and ultimately – the survival of the organization. That is why from the perspective of BSE, crisis management is an extremely important process in organization, as it is directly aimed at achieving the realignment after changes, which occur within the environment and organization itself.

There are multiple models, which have been constructed to show all the aspects of crisis management processes within the organization, being based on the models of the stages of crisis (Elsubbaugh, Fildes, & Rose, 2004; Pearson & Claire, 1998; Shrivastava, 1995; Mitroff, 2005). One of the most representative models was presented by Mitroff (2005), which remains in line with the proposed 4 stages of crisis. Mitroff (2005) proposed following stages of crisis management: signal detection, probing/preparation, containment/damage limitation, business recovery, no fault learning, redesign. Pearson and Mitroff (2019) are stating that the preparations which should be performed by the organizations in order to achieve the effective crisis management should concern various crisis-response connected capabilities from every organizational element, which may somehow contribute to organizational survival:

(a) technical, (b) human factor, (c) infrastructural, (d) cultural, and (e) emotional/belief. Authors are underlining the role of technical element, as they are stating that they are the "mechanisms that organize company work-specific tasks and the materials and equipment necessary to support task completion. The availability and condition of tools and equipment and the existence of alarms and shut-down mechanisms are critical considerations" (Pearson & Mitroff, 2019). Therefore, it seems that IT may play a vital role in crisis management and that role should be studied further to understand whether there are indeed mechanisms, which allow organizations operating under conditions caused by BSE to benefit from IT use.

1.2.3 COVID-19 as a specific example of Black Swan event

The pandemic outbreaks existed even before there was a possibility for their coherent analysis and for modern society, they almost always marked a significant development moment in the world (Donthu & Gustafsson, 2020). Also, the researchers and practitioners are not debating that the next pandemic will happen someday, and the efforts are solely focused on determining when it will be (Stöhr & Esveld, 2004). Historically, global pandemics seem to "occur at 10–50-year intervals as a result of the emergence of new virus subtypes from virus re-assortment" (Donthu & Gustafsson, 2020). With the increase of global populations and the territory needed for supporting this increase, it seems that such pandemics will happen more often than less.

Donthu and Gustafsson (2020) stated that the COVID-19 pandemic outbreak has forced many organizations into crisis and the vast amount of them not recovered from it.

The pandemic of COVID-19, which started at the beginning of 2020 and its waves are still present (even though the vaccination limited its negative effects), is considered by most scholars as one of the most devastating crises of contemporary world, with long-term profound consequences for entire economies, various industries, organizations, and employees all over the world (Choudhury, Koo, & Li, 2020; Margherita, Elia, & Klein, 2021; Tønnessen, Dhir, & Flåten, 2021). According to the WHO report from March 2021 (WHO, 2022), approximately 600 million people have been infected with COVID-19 globally and more than 6.5 million people have died because of it. Specific characteristics of the COVID-19 pandemic are given in Table 1.2. According to Dwivedi et al. (2020) "for many business leaders and managers, COVID-19 is the most disruptive, world-changing event in living memory".

From the perspective of management sciences, it is important to state that various researchers considered the COVID-19 pandemic to be a cause for a deep economic crisis, which was a source of declining economic growth and deteriorating prospects for employees (Baert et al., 2020; OECD, 2020; Tønnessen, Dhir, & Flåten, 2021). This, in turn, caused global economic

Table 1.2 The COVID-19 pandemic timeline

Date	*Place/ Organization*	*Action*
December 12, 2019	China, Hubei, Wuhan	First report of atypical pneumonia illness
December 30, 2019	China, Hubei, Wuhan	The World Health Organization (WHO) Country Office in China is informed of several cases of pneumonia of unknown etiology
January 2, 2020	WHO	WHO activates its Incident Management Support Team (IMST)
January 10, 2020	WHO	WHO announces that the outbreak in Wuhan, China is caused by the 2019 Novel Coronavirus (2019-nCoV).
January 10, 2020	CDC	CDC publishes information about the 2019 Novel Coronavirus (2019-nCoV) on its website.
January 12, 2020	China	China publicly shares the genetic sequence of COVID-19
January 13, 2020	Thailand	First case of COVID-19 outside of China
January 22, 2020	WHO	WHO announces Emergency Committee (EC) under the International Health Regulations (IHR 2005)
February 3, 2020	WHO	WHO releases the international community's Strategic Preparedness and Response Plan
March 11, 2020	WHO	WHO declares COVID-19 a pandemic
April 2, 2020	Worldwide	1 million cases of COVID-19 worldwide
December 14, 2020	Worldwide	COVID-19 Alpha variant detected
December 20, 2020	Worldwide	COVID-19 Delta variant detected
November 24, 2021	Worldwide	COVID-19 Omicron variant detected
August 11, 2020	Russia	Announcement of Sputnik V – first COVID-19 vaccine, which received regulatory approval
November 9, 2020	Worldwide	Announcement of Comirnaty – Pfizer / BioNtech COVID-19 mRNA vaccine development with 90% of preventing illness
December 18, 2020	Worldwide	Announcement of Moderna COVID-19 mRNA vaccine development with 93% of preventing illness
December 8, 2020	Worldwide	Announcement of AstraZeneca (developed by University of Oxford) COVID-19 vaccine development with 74% of preventing symptomatic illness
February 27, 2021	Worldwide	Announcement of Johnson & Johnson COVID-19 single-dosage vaccine development with 72% of preventing symptomatic illness

Source: https://www.nytimes.com/interactive/2020/science/coronavirus-vaccine-tracker.html

downturn and rising fears of unemployment (Christelis et al., 2021; Dosi & Soete, 2022). Various research connected with the changes occurring in the world at the beginning of the COVID-19 pandemic described negative implications of the control measures, which were introduced around the world (Goodell, 2020; Mimoun, Ben Ari, & Margalit, 2020; Tønnessen, Dhir, & Flåten, 2021; Usher, 2020). Almost all countries implemented specific regulations in order to contain the spread of the COVID-19 pandemic while vaccinations were not available, including lockdown (partial or total), self-isolation, social distancing, and work from home (Davison, 2020; Tønnessen, Dhir, & Flåten, 2021; Yoo & Managi, 2020). It is fully possible that the slogan "stay at home" will forever remain the best description of the change, which happened around the world at the beginning of XXI century.

It is hard to assign the COVID-19 pandemic to a specific type of BSE. Shepherd and Williams (2020) proposed a theoretical framework, which distinguished between adverse events (e.g., earthquakes or terrorist acts) and persistent adversity (e.g., poverty), offering a division between an event happening in a specific point of time from an event happening continuously. During the first wave of the COVID-19 pandemic, looking at the unpredictability of the situation, its development (also lack of the ability to predict the end of it), and shock, which was connected with it Otrachshenko et al. (2022), it was treated as the persistent event, happening continuously without the specific point of time of its end. The development of the COVID-19 pandemic confirmed such assignment, as indeed it was clear that the pandemic was not limited to the specific and a short point in time, as it remained a source of crisis for the entire world over the next years. When the BSE is a one-time shock, pinpointed in a specific point in time, employees usually respond by falling into some chronic dysfunction or engaging in innovative entrepreneurial action (Shepherd & Williams, 2020). In case of the COVID-19 pandemic and the fact that finally it was a persistent event, falling into chronic dysfunction became impossible, as it would be a clear reason for organization collapse. Therefore, there was a clear need to innovate and change the way, in which organizations operate.

1.3 IT in crisis

There are not a lot of studies, which aim directly at the analysis of IT role in avoiding or surviving crisis caused by various events (including BSE, but not limiting to them). The literature coverage is usually connected to crisis management and IT stays at the background of all considerations offered by authors (Leidner, Pan, & Pan, 2009).

Resource Based View (RBW), usually adopted in case of the analysis of IT in organization, is helpful also in this case. It seems to be an effective theoretical lens, which allows to understand what is the role of IT in organization, which is experiencing crisis. Leidner, Pan, and Pan (2009) underlined three main approaches to IT support under such circumstances, which are conducive for obtaining benefits from it:

- IT should be treated as a central resource in crisis response.
- IT should be viewed in the context of other central resources to "uncover the complementarities needed for IT to pave the way toward quick crisis response".
- IT should be used for the coordination of the deployment of other resources in crisis response.

It is well-known fact that any resource may influence other resources in the organization in three ways: compensatory, enhancing, and suppressing (Wade & Hulland, 2004). The literature coverage confirming that IT has the potential to be a resource which enhances other non-IT resources in organization is still very poor; however, authors agree that it has a great potential for those technologies for organizations operating under crisis (Wade & Hulland, 2004). As crisis situation by their definition is unstable, the coordination and reconfiguration of the resources becomes a critical issue (Thomas & Fritz, 2006). Therefore, the findings of Leidner, Pan, & Pan (2009) should be treated as important conclusions in this regard.

However, such enhancement may also appear due to limiting some problems, which arise in organization due to the crisis. The role of IT support for organizations operating under crisis is also directly connected to its ability to limit various shortcomings of organizations, which are appearing in such conditions. Comfort (1993) discusses three perspectives connected to overcoming limitations in "human information processing", which are usually connected to the organizations functioning in dynamic and turbulent environments, characterized by quick and unpredictable changes. IT support is conducive for the development of an interactive network of disaster managers, which facilitates quick communication and allows to focus overall attention on all problems, which are identified in various places. IT also allows to present gathered information in simplified, graphic, or systemic way, which may be conducive for their fast dissemination and supports the accuracy of communication. Finally, IT allows to develop and organize 'extended memory', which may be also considered a knowledge base allowing to store and process all information connected to specific event or relevant for specific group of employees. It shows another perspective, which offers important conclusions in this regard.

Leidner, Pan, and Pan (2009) confirmed that IT structure, next to organizational and information structure, was key for deploying and reconfiguring resources and capabilities in organizations to respond to the crisis. However, they confirmed after other authors (Weill, 2004), that a specific "IT monarchy" is needed to achieve such benefits and the role of IT during crisis is so important that decisions concerning its use should be centralized and considered to have a strategic character.

Therefore, it is not surprising that many authors underline the role of IT during crisis, stating that "the control of each phase of the crisis can be reached or facilitated using IT" (Asadzadeh et al., 2020). Empirical evidence offered in the literature indicate that IT support is useful in each phase of the crisis, particularly underlining its importance in the response phase (Reddick, 2011; Sakurai & Murayama, 2019; Tom-Aba et al., 2015).

1.3.1 *IT during crisis caused by BSE*

The issue of IT use in organization was previously heavily discussed in the literature from the point of view of various BSE. Vast amount of previous literature studies confirmed the overall beneficial impacts of IT on the organizations functioning under difficult conditions caused by various BSE, connected to global health, poverty alleviation, climate change, humanitarian crises, and natural disasters (e.g. Braa, Monteiro, & Sahay, 2004; Heeks & Arun, 2010; Rajão & Hayes, 2009; Tim et al., 2017; Tusiime & Byrne, 2011).

Various authors are connecting the issue of Black Swan events and a crisis caused by such with disaster recovery, stating that there are the same stages, based on which the organizations would go through when the conditions of BSE start to influence its performance. Based on the work of (Sakurai & Murayama, 2019), there are four stages of disaster recovery: risk reduction, preparedness, response, and recovery. It is visible that those stages resemble the stages of crisis occurring in the organization. Hence, any conclusions made concerning the IT importance for organization may also be useful from the point of view of organization experiencing crisis.

Sakurai and Murayama (2019) are stating that first of all, IT allows employees to record, exchange, and process any disaster-related information (in this case – BSE-related information) throughout four disaster management stages. At the stage of risk assessment, it allows for monitoring risk in real-time. At the stage of preparedness, it allows for scenario simulations and creating a knowledge repository. At the stage of response, it provides various situational information in real-time. At the stage of recovery, it allows to manage any recovery actions and redesign of way of operating. Moreover, Aldunce et al. (2015) are stating that such actions are strengthening situational awareness, which is crucial in shaping any response of organization for the changes occurring within the environment.

Such statements allow to conclude that IT support during crisis caused by BSE is even more important. Due to lack of time and extremely high speed of changes and high level of their unpredictability connected to BSE, the positive influence of IT connected to resource allocation and reconfiguration and limiting the problems occurring within the organization (discussed in case of any crisis) will be much greater.

1.3.2 *IT during crisis caused by specific BSE – the COVID-19 pandemic*

The issue of IT support for organizations operating under the critical conditions caused by a specific BSE – COVID-19 is quite unique and should be analyzed in full independently. Vahdat (2021) underlines that organizations faced "an extraordinary threat, one that pushes them to delve into uncharted terrain and handle it directly while changing their workers in unprecedented technological, physical and socio-psychological ways". He underlined that the level of digital transformation forced all organizations to embrace IT. The COVID-19 pandemic created a potential for the enormous rise in the speed of digitalization of contemporary organizations, fostering new opportunities for their development (Ciarli et al., 2021; Dosi & Soete, 2022) and further underlining the importance of IT support for organizations operating under crisis. Various countries reported rise of entrepreneurship connected with new solutions to support and development for contemporary organizations, underlining that those organizations decided to use that opportunity and make a step into a new business environment, which started to arise (Altun et al., 2021).

The role of IT during and after the COVID-19 pandemic is widely discussed in the literature, as IT was a key for surviving the pandemic itself due to the specific character of COVID-19, an example of BSE (Davison, 2020). Various researchers indicate that the COVID-19 pandemic caused an exponential boost in the use of IT among organizations forced to innovate and change – through reconfiguration of their resources and redesign (Chandra, Shirish, & Srivastava, 2020; Savić, 2020; Tønnessen, Dhir, & Flåten, 2021). Davison (2020) stated that the pandemic of COVID-19 changed many aspects of everyday lives of the 21st century employees and underlined that especially the areas connected with IT use in organizations (such as e.g. information behavior, business models, cybersecurity, and data privacy) underwent huge reinvention. It is also underlined by Pan and Zhang (2020) that: "While many organizations began to develop strategies for a digital workplace before the COVID-19 pandemic, the outbreak of the disease has forced most organizations to launch new initiatives that enable them to accelerate the transformation to the digital workplace" (Caligiuri et al., 2020). Many other researchers confirm that unprecedented strength of the COVID-19 pandemic influence on organizations, forced to realign to the rapidly changing conditions of functioning.

In the context of this study, the notion of IT is limited to IT used by organizations in order to fulfill their goals. Therefore, the positive and negative influences of IT on managing and suppressing the pandemic itself are not important here, even though those are usually described in various articles concerning IT role during the COVID-19 pandemic. The literature coverage of the issues regarding IT is mainly connected to (Dwivedi et al., 2021):

- Education and IT support for online teaching and learning.
- Health sector and IT support for online healthcare.
- Supply chain redesign.
- Transition into work from home concept.
- Information management and data visualization concerning pandemic itself.

However, there is an important conclusion coming from this extensive body of literature: crisis caused by the COVID-19 pandemic has a different impact on organization and the level and depth of this impact is depending on the degree of digitalization of tasks activities and the contribution of IT in creating value for organization (Dwivedi et al., 2020)). Moreover, not only the level of IT-dependence of the specific organization is important here but also the level of IT-dependence of entire industry, in which this organization operates (Constantiou, Marton, & Tuunainen, 2017).

Moreover, it must be shown that the positive influence of IT on the entire economy may cause various effects for each organization separately and may also cause some negative effects. The best example here is the issue connected with work from home concept, which is understood as a practice in which employees are able to carry out their work-related activities from their home instead of the place of employment at the employer's office, using IT (Allen, Golden, & Shockley, 2015). The possibility of working from home gave entire economy a great advantage, allowing various businesses to continue their operations through various limitations imposed in almost every country in the world (social distancing, stay-at-home restrictions). However, from the point of view of organization, positive aspects of such change may be seen (Lourel et al., 2009). The work from home concept changed the dynamic of employees' cooperation and work management (Rioveros et al., 2021; Tønnessen, Dhir, & Flåten, 2021). At first, various positive aspects were correlated with that, and it turned out that employees are able to maintain their job performance even while working remotely. In time, the negative effects of such change started, showing increased anxiety (Usher, 2020), stress (Mimoun, Ben Ari, & Margalit, 2020), and productivity loss (Goodell, 2020). It caused the need for developing new human resource strategies (Bieńkowska et al., 2022) in order to mitigate those negative effects and redesign the way the IT is utilize in the organization.

It should also be stated that the redesign of the IT use during the COVID-19 pandemic is significantly different from any other the pre-COVID-19 pandemic or probably post-COVID-19 changes because of three aspects: unprecedented scale (Tønnessen, Dhir, & Flåten, 2021), rapid introduction (Dwivedi et al., 2020), and enforcement (Waizenegger et al., 2020). Organizations were forced to quickly implement a variety of IT solutions (new IT or redesign of existing IT) to maintain their continuity and uninterrupted service to their customers (Hines et al., 2020). Therefore, the changes which occurred within the organizations to realign the IT with changed needs were not voluntary and developed in usual quality-ensuring circles of implementation. That is why they were a source of very specific changes introduced with unprecedented rapidity.

It all shows that the analysis of existing body of literature concerning the use of IT in organizations during and after the COVID-19 pandemic is an extremely difficult task, as it is needed to carefully assess each conclusion, determining whether it is relevant from such point of view. Any simple systemic literature review and scholars databases searches themselves are not

Table 1.3 Literature coverage of IT support during COVID-19

Variables analyzed in the study	*Source*
Organizational culture, job satisfaction, IT	Sapta, Muafi, and Setini (2021)
Effective HRM, IT	Rahman et al. (2020)
HRM functions, IT	Aurelia and Momin (2020)
Digitalized crisis response, IT	Guo et al. (2020)
Human ingenuity, innovation, IT	Bruce (2020)
Performance efficiency, IT	Rahman et al. (2020)
HRM, IT	Saxena, Bagga, and Gupta (2021)
Work from home, IT	Agrawal, Pani, and Sharma (2020); Prasada, Vaidya, and Mangipudic (2020)
Remote working, IT	Islam et al. (2020); Belzunegui-Eraso and Erro-Garces (2020)
Organizational support for HRM, IT	Gigauri (2020)

enough, as the careful consideration of each contribution is needed. The main literature coverage is shown in Table 1.3, underlining the need to analyze IT in the context of its influence on employees and their performance, not only the performance of the organization as a whole.

Several renowned researchers from the field of IT use in organizations have contributed to that field of study analyzing the role of IT for contemporary organizations during the COVID-19 pandemic. Even though in almost all contributions there is a mix of perspectives on IT (and an organization perspective should be the only one considered here), it is possible to formulate valid conclusions. Their analysis is offering key conclusions, which are highly relevant for underlining the importance of this study:

- The COVID-19 pandemic has forced to reassess the use of IT in contemporary organizations.
- The introduction of artificial intelligence algorithms could engender better, more informed decision-making under critical conditions.
- IT is directly connected to the issues of privacy and security, which are arising due to more extensive use of IT.

Pan and Zhang (2020) identified six themes of research from the field of IT around which new topics are arising from the beginning of the COVID-19 pandemic. There are: 'expanding digital surveillance', 'tackling the infodemic', 'orchestrating data ecosystems', 'adapting information behaviors', 'developing the digital workplace', and 'maintaining social distancing'. Those groups were aggregated in two dimensions, that are: 'fighting against a pandemic' and 'adjusting to a new normal'. From the purpose of this study, the dimension 'adjusting to a new normal' seems to be the one to be considered carefully.

1.3.3 IT after the COVID-19 pandemic

The existing body of literature shows that the world will likely not go back to the way it was before the COVID-19 pandemic. The search in the ScienceDirect database of the phrase "COVID-19" and "new normal" shows 2295 articles published in years 2021–2023. It shows that both researchers and practitioners are already preparing themselves for existing in this new, transformed business environment. As stated by Pan and Zhang (2020), "certain new environments may become a new normal for people worldwide". Such statement is especially true for IT use in organizations. It should not be treated as a negative effect of the COVID-19 pandemic, because organizations have made an awfully big step forward on the road for more efficient IT support that it would be a waste to even think about making a step back from it. The COVID-19 pandemic, which is not yet over, causes a new digitalized business world to arise and tackling the issue of crises caused by next waves of the COVID-19 pandemic or various different BSEs is an especially valid research gap. To summarize such line of though, the following statement may be recalled: "Since we are not in a position to foresee how COVID-19 pandemic will evolve in the future, but we can anticipate future similar challenges, businesses should reconsider their digitalization strategy by focusing on exploiting the underlying opportunities in the near future" (Dwivedi et al., 2020).

The perspective of employees who are the ones using such IT on a daily basis seems to also be important here. Milasi et al. (2020) underlined that 30–40% of non-manual workers in most Eastern European countries lack digital skills, which is generating an enormous problem in the context of their functioning in the "new normal" arising after the COVID-19 pandemic. However, the global survey concerning employees from almost 190 countries (Strack et al., 2021) showed that almost two in three employees is committed to learn new skills to seek for a new job which will offer them more security and opportunities to develop, for which those digital skills are crucial. Moreover, "most workers who wanted to learn new skills for a new job did so because they wanted to switch to IT or digital jobs" (Strack et al., 2021). Therefore, employees are also seeing the trends, which are arising in the 21st century after the COIVD-19 pandemic and their commitment to align their carriers with these trends also show that the new much more IT-dependent world, with significantly higher dynamics and unpredictability of the environment is the one, in which we all be living.

1.4 New understanding of IT support after BSE – the COVID-19 pandemic

Various researchers tried to offer some insights into the post-COVID-19 world and the much more significant role of IT in it (Almeida, Santos, & Monteiro, 2020; Barnes, 2020; Nadikattu, 2020). Nadikattu (2020) stated that the world was rebooted and now we need to look at it from fully different perspective, especially in management studies.

Digital business transformation is the concept, which arose in the literature at the beginning of the 21st century, gained even more importance during the COVID-19 pandemic, as it concerned the biggest change, which is occurring in the environment of contemporary organizations. Martin (2008) defined digital business transformation as the use of IT not in cases of trivial automation of processes, but "in the case where fundamentally new capabilities are created in business, public government, and in the lives of people and society". Liu, Chen, and Chou (2011) added that "digital transformation is an organizational transformation that integrates digital technologies and business processes in a digital economy", which is consistent with the views of Solis et al. (2014) stating that it "is the realignment of, or new investment in, technology and business models". Digital business transformation is particularly connected with organizations and the arising role of IT within their scope of operations; thus, Liu, Chen, and Chou (2011) is underlining its role in organizational transformation, which is "a complex, revolutionary, and continuous process that demands fundamental changes in the organizational structures and systems leading to reassessments of organizational norms and values". Such digital transformation caused the new perspective on IT to arise, showing that scholars and practitioners are no longer analyzing the sole issue of IT support existence in contemporary organizations.

Hence, the literature analysis showed that the importance of IT use in organization has risen over the last decades, only to further increase the speed of this increase due to the COVID-19 pandemic. The benefits obtained from the use of IT discussed in the literature before the COVID-19 pandemic are beginning to be seen as a cornerstone needed for the continuity of business of contemporary organizations. Moreover, the organizations are forced to operate in the environment characterized by:

- higher level of unpredictability and dynamics, causing crisis to occur more easily and less predictably,
- higher level of digitalization, causing organizations to rely much more on IT support.

That fact itself causes the need to redefine the existing approach to the analysis of IT in organization and identify new mechanisms, which cause IT support to contribute to overall organizational performance, also in case of crisis avoidance and survival.

Literature

't Hart, P., Rosenthal, U., & Kouzmin, A. (1993). Crisis decision making: The centralization thesis revisited. *Administration & Society*, 25(1), 12–45.

't Hart, P., Heyse, L., & Boin, A. (2001). New trends in crisis management practice and crisis management research: Setting the agenda. *Journal of Contingencies and Crisis Management*, 9(4), 181–188.

Accomazzo, D., & Rivadeneyra, R. (2009). *An alternative way to manage equity portfolios*. Graziadio Business Report, Graziadio School of Business and Management, Pepperdine University, 12(1), 2259–2279.

Aceto, G., Persico, V., & Pescapé, A. (2019). A survey on information and communication technologies for industry 4.0: State-of-the-art, taxonomies, perspectives, and challenges. *IEEE Communications Surveys & Tutorials*, 21(4), 3467–3501.

Agarwal, R., & Prasad, J. (1997). The role of innovation characteristics and perceived voluntariness in the acceptance of information technologies. *Decision Sciences*, 28(3), 557–582.

Agrawal, K. P., Pani, A. K., & Sharma, R. (2020). Pandemic pandemonium and remote working: an investigation of determinants and their contextual behavior in virtualization of work-from- home (WFH) process. *Paper Presented at the International Working Conference on Transfer and Diffusion of IT.*

Ajibade, P. (2018). Technology acceptance model limitations and criticisms: Exploring the practical applications and use in technology-related studies, mixed-method, and qualitative researches. *Library Philosophy and Practice*, 9, 1–13.

Aldunce, P., Beilin, R., Howden, M., & Handmer, J. (2015). Resilience for disaster risk management in a changing climate: Practitioners' frames and practices. *Global Environmental Change*, 30, 1–11.

Allen, T. D., Golden, T. D., & Shockley, K. M. (2015). How effective is telecommuting? Assessing the status of our scientific findings. *Psychological Science in the Public Interest*, 16(2), 40–68.

Almeida, F., Santos, J. D., & Monteiro, J. A. (2020). The challenges and opportunities in the digitalization of companies in a post-COVID-19 World. *IEEE Engineering Management Review*, 48(3), 97–103.

Altun, T., Akyıldız, S., Gülay, A., & Özdemir, C. (2021). Investigating education faculty students' views about asynchronous distance education practices during Covid-19 isolation period. *Psycho-Educational Research Reviews*, 34–45.

Asadzadeh, A., Pakkhoo, S., Saeidabad, M. M., Khezri, H., & Ferdousi, R. (2020). Information technology in emergency management of COVID-19 outbreak. *Informatics in Medicine Unlocked*, 21, 100475.

Attaran, M. (2003). Information technology and business-process redesign. *Business Process Management Journal*, 9(4), 440–458.

Atzori, L., Iera, A., & Morabito, G. (2010). The internet of things: A survey. *Computer Networks*, 54(15), 2787–2805.

Aurelia, S., & Momin, M. M. (2020). Global reverberation and prediction for HRM amid and after COVID-19: A technological viewpoint. *Materials Today: Proceedings*, 46, 1–13.

Baert, S., Lippens, L., Moens, E., Weytjens, J., & Sterkens, P. (2020). The COVID-19 crisis and telework: A research survey on experiences, expectations and hopes. *The European Journal of Health Economics*, 23(4), 729–753.

Bagozzi, R. P. (2007). The legacy of technology acceptance model and a proposal for a paradigm shift. *Journal of the Association for Information Systems*, 8(4), 244–254.

Bailey, J. E., & Pearson, S. W. (1983). Development of a tool for measuring and analyzing computer user satisfaction. *Management Science*, 29(5), 530–545.

Bakos, J. Y., & Treacy, M. E. (1986). Information technology and corporate strategy: A research perspective. *MIS Quarterly*, 124, 107–119.

Barnes, S. J. (2020). Information management research and practice in the post-COVID-19 world. *International Journal of Information Management*, 55, 102175.

Belzunegui-Eraso, A., & Erro-Garces, A. (2020). Teleworking in the context of the covid-19 crisis. *Sustainability*, 12(9), 3662.

Benbya, H., Pachidi, S., & Jarvenpaa, S. (2021). Special issue editorial: Artificial intelligence in organizations: implications for information systems research. *Journal of the Association for Information Systems*, 22(2), 10.

Bergeron, F., & Raymond, L. (1995). The contribution of IT to the bottom line: a contingency perspective of strategic dimensions. In *Proceedings of the Sixteenth International Conference on Information Systems Dec 10–13, 1995, Amsterdam*: 167–181.

Best, M. (2001). *The new competitive advantage: The renewal of American industry*. Oxford: Oxford University Press.

Bieńkowska, A., Koszela, A., Sałamacha, A., & Tworek, K. (2022). COVID-19 oriented HRM strategies influence on job and organizational performance through job-related attitudes. *PLOS One*, 17(4), e0266364.

Boar, B. H. (1997). *Strategic thinking for information technology: How to build the IT organization for the information age*. New York: John Wiley & Sons.

Bonomi, F., Milito, R., Zhu, J., & Addepalli, S. (2012). *Fog computing and its role in the Internet of Things*. Proceedings of ACM 1st Ed. MCC Workshop Mobile Cloud Computer (pp. 13–16).

Borgmann, A. (2006). Technology as a cultural force for Alena and Griffin. *The Canadian Journal of Sociology/Cahiers canadiens de sociologie*, 31(3), 351–360.

Boudreaux, B. J. (2005). Exploring a multi-stage model of crisis management: Utilities, hurricanes, and contingency (Doctoral dissertation, University of Florida).

Braa, J., Monteiro, E., & Sahay, S. (2004). Networks of action: Sustainable health information systems across developing countries. *MIS Quarterly*, 28(3), 337–362.

Bruce, T. (2020). Corona Virus Disease (COVID 19): Rapid human ingenuity through innovation and technology as a proactive and admirable response in the storm of a global pandemic. Preprint doi: 10.13140/RG.2.2.25262.46405/3.

Caligiuri, P., De Cieri, H., Minbaeva, D., Verbeke, A., & Zimmermann, A. (2020). International HRM insights for navigating the COVID-19 pandemic: Implications for future research and practice. *Journal of International Business Studies*, 51(5), 697–713.

Carbonara, N. (2005). Information and communication technology and geographical clusters: Opportunities and spread. *Technovation*, 25(3), 213–222.

Card, S., Moran, T., & Newell, A. (1986). The model human processor—An engineering model of human performance. In *Handbook of Perception and Human Performance*: 45–49, vol. 2. New York: Wiley.

Carr, A. S., & Smeltzer, L. R. (2002). The relationship between information technology use and buyer-supplier relationships: An exploratory analysis of the buying firm's perspective. *IEEE Transactions on Engineering Management*, 49(3), 293–304.

Cetindamar, D., Phaal, R., & Probert, D. (2009). Understanding technology management as a dynamic capability: A framework for technology management activities. *Technovation*, 29(4), 237–246.

Chan, F. K. Y., Thong, J. Y. L., Venkatesh, V., Brown, S. A., Hu, P. J., & Tam, K. Y. (2010). Modeling citizen satisfaction with mandatory adoption of an e-government technology. *Journal of the Association for Information Systems*, 11(10), 519–549.

Chan, S. L. (2000). Information technology in business processes. *Business Process Management Journal*, 6(3).

Chandra, S., Shirish, A., & Srivastava, S. C. (2020). Theorizing technological spatial intrusion for ICT enabled employee innovation: The mediating role of perceived usefulness. *Technological Forecasting and Social Change*, 161, 120320.

Chen, M., Mao, S., & Liu, Y. (2014). Big data: A survey. *Mobile Networks and Application*, 19(2), 171–209.

Cheney, P. H., Mann, R. I., & Amoroso, D. L. (1986). Organizational factors affecting the success of end-user computing. *Journal of Management Information Systems*, 3(1), 65–80.

Choudhury, P., Koo, W. W., & Li, X. (2020). Working (from home) during a crisis: Online social contributions by workers during the coronavirus shock. Harvard Business School Technology & Operations Management Unit Working Paper (20-096).

Christelis, D., Georgarakos, D., Jappelli, T., & Kenny, G. (2021). How has COVID-19 crisis affected different households' consumption in the euro area. *ECB Research Bulletin*, (84), 1–6.

Ciarli, T., Kenney, M., Massini, S., & Piscitello, L. (2021). Digital technologies, innovation, and skills: Emerging trajectories and challenges. *Research Policy*, 50(7), 104289.

Comfort, L. K. (1993). Integrating information technology into international crisis management and policy. *Journal of Contingencies and Crisis Management*, 1(1), 15–26.

Constantiou, I., Marton, A., & Tuunainen, V. K. (2017). Four models of sharing economy platforms. *MIS Quarterly Executive*, 16(4), 231–251.

Coombs, R., Knights, D., & Willmott, H. C. (1992). Culture, control and competition; towards a conceptual framework for the study of information technology in organizations. *Organization Studies*, 13(1), 51–72.

Coombs, W. T. (1999). Information and compassion in crisis responses: A test of their effects. *Journal of Public Relations Research*, 11(2), 125–142.

Cortada, J. W. (2019). Rethinking why and how organizations acquire information technologies, Part 1. *IEEE Annals of the History of Computing*, 41(4), 48–60.

Cotec, P. (1998). A guide to technology management and innovation for companies, EC Project, Bruksela.

Croteau, A. M., & Bergeron, F. (2001). An information technology trilogy: Business strategy, technological deployment and organizational performance. *The Journal of Strategic Information Systems*, 10(2), 77–99.

Crowston, K., Sawyer, S., & Wigand, R. (2001). Investigating the interplay between structure and information and communications technology in the real estate industry. *Information Technology & People*, 14(2), 163–183.

Daft, R. L. (2007). *Organization theory and design*. Thomson South-Western, Mason.

Das, S. R., Zahra, S. A., & Warkentin, M. E. (1991). Integrating the content and process of strategic MIS planning with competitive strategy. *Decision Sciences*, 22(5), 953–984.

Davis, F. D. (1985). A technology acceptance model for empirically testing new end-user information systems: Theory and results (Doctoral dissertation, Massachusetts Institute of Technology).

Davison, C. (2020). Stock returns, leverage, and the COVID-19 pandemic. Available at SSRN.

Davison, R. M. (2020). The transformative potential of disruptions: A viewpoint. *International Journal of Information Management*, 55, 102149.

DeLone, W. H., & McLean, E. R. (2003). The DeLone and McLean model of information systems success: A ten-year update. *Journal of Management Information Systems*, 19(4), 9–30.

DeNardis, L. (2010). The emerging field of Internet governance. Yale Information Society Project, Working Paper Series.

DePietro, R., Wiarda, E., & Fleischer, M. (1990). The context for change: Organization, technology and environment. In L. G. Tornatzky & M. Fleischer (Eds.), *The processes of technological innovation* (pp. 151–175). Lexington, MA: Lexington Books.

DeSanctis, G., & Poole, M. S. (1994). Capturing the complexity in advanced technology use: Adaptive structuration theory. *Organization Science*, 5(2), 121–147.

Dewett, T., & Jones, G. R. (2001). The role of information technology in the organization: A review, model, and assessment. *Journal of Management*, 27(3), 313–346.

Dhillon, G., & Backhouse, J. (1996). Risks in the use of information technology within organizations. *International Journal of Information Management*, 16(1), 65–74.

Dillon, A. (2001). User acceptance of information technology. *Encyclopedia of Human Factors and Ergonomics*, 1, 1105–1109.

Dogson, M. (2000). The management of technological innovation. Oxford: Oxford University Press.

Dohale, V., Gunasekaran, A., Akarte, M. M., & Verma, P. (2020), Twenty-five years' contribution of 'Benchmarking: an International Journal' to manufacturing strategy: A scientometric review. *Benchmarking: An International Journal*, 27(10), 2887–2908.

Donthu, N., & Gustafsson, A. (2020). Effects of COVID-19 on business and research. *Journal of Business Research*, 117, 284–289.

Dosi, G., & Soete, L. (2022). On the syndemic nature of crises: A Freeman perspective. *Research Policy*, 51(1), 104393.

Dwivedi, Y. K., Hughes, D. L., Coombs, C., Constantiou, I., Duan, Y., Edwards, J. S., ... & Upadhyay, N. (2020). Impact of COVID-19 pandemic on information management research and practice: Transforming education, work and life. *International Journal of Information Management*, 55, 102211.

Ellis, C. A., Gibbs, S. J., & Rein, G. (1991). Groupware: Some issues and experiences. *Communications of the ACM*, 34(1), 39–58.

Elsubbaugh, S., Fildes, R., & Rose, M. B. (2004). Preparation for crisis management: A proposed model and empirical evidence. *Journal of Contingencies and Crisis Management*, 12(3), 112–127.

Falkheimer, J., & Heide, M. (2006). Multicultural crisis communication: Towards a social constructionist perspective. *Journal of Contingencies and Crisis Management*, 14(4), 180–189.

Feller, J., & Fitzgerald, B. (2000). A framework analysis of the open source software development paradigm. In *Proceedings of 21st Annual International Conference on Information Systems*, pp. 58–69.

Fink, S., & American Management Association. (1986). Crisis management: Planning for the inevitable. Amacom.

Flage, R., & Aven, T. (2015). Emerging risk–Conceptual definition and a relation to black swan type of events. *Reliability Engineering & System Safety*, 144, 61–67.

Galbraith, J. R. (2014). Organizational design challenges resulting from big data. *Journal of Organization Design*, 3(1), 2–13.

Gierszewska G. & Romanowska M. (2003). Analiza strategiczna Przedsiębiorstwa. Polskie Wydawnictwo Ekonomiczne, Warszawa.

Gigauri, I. (2020). Organizational support to HRM in times of the COVID-19 pandemic crisis. *European Journal of Marketing and Economics*, 3(3), 36–48.

Goodell, J. W. (2020). COVID-19 and finance: Agendas for future research. *Finance Research Letters*, 35, 101512.

Goodhue, D. L., & Thompson, R. L. (1995). Task-technology fit and individual performance. *MIS Quarterly*, 19(2), 213–236.

Green, L. W., & Kreuter, M. W. (1999). *Health promotion planning: An educational and ecological approach*. Mountain View, CA: Mayfield.

Gregory, M. J. (1995). Technology management: A process approach. *Proceedings of the Institution of Mechanical Engineers, Part B: Journal of Engineering Manufacture*, 209(5), 347–356.

Gundel, S. (2005). Towards anew typology of crises. *Journal of Contingencies and Crisis Management*, 13(3), 106–115.

Guo, H., Yang, Z., Huang, R., & Guo, A. (2020). The digitalization and public crisis responses of small and medium enterprises: Implications from a COVID-19 survey. *Frontiers of Business Research in China*, 14(1), 1–25.

Heeks, R., & Arun, S. (2010). Social outsourcing as a development tool: The impact of outsourcing IT services to women's social enterprises in Kerala. *Journal of International Development: The Journal of the Development Studies Association*, 22(4), 441–454.

Henderson, J., & Venkatraman, N. (1993). Strategic alignment: Leveraging information technology for transforming organizations. *IBM Systems Journal*, 32(1), 4–16.

Henderson, J. C., & Venkatraman, H. (1999). Strategic alignment: Leveraging information technology for transforming organizations. *IBM Systems Journal*, 38(2.3), 472–484.

Higgins, D. M. (2014). Fires, floods and financial meltdowns: Black swan events and property asset management. Property Management, Emerald Group Publishing, School of Property Construction and Project Management, RMIT University, Melbourne, 32(3), 241–255.

Hines, S. E., Chin, K. H., Levine, A. R., & Wickwire, E. M. (2020). Initiation of a survey of healthcare worker distress and moral injury at the onset of the COVID-19 surge. *American Journal of Industrial Medicine*.

Hollander, A., & E. Denna, et al. (1999). Accounting, information technology, and business solutions. Irwin: McGraw-Hill Higher Education.

Hu, Q., & Huang, C. (2005). Aligning IT with firm business strategies using the balance scorecard system, in proceedings of the 38th Annual Hawaii International Conference on System Sciences. Hawaii: HICSS, pp. 1–10.

Hutchby, I. (1995). Aspects of recipient design in expert advice-giving on call-in radio. *Discourse Processes*, 19(2), 219–238.

Islam, M. A., Igwe, P. A., Rahman, M., & Saif, A. N. M. (2020). Remote working challenges and solutions: insights from SMEs in Bangladesh during the COVID-19 pandemic. *International Journal of Quality and Innovation*, 5, 119–140.

Ivanova, I. A., Pulyaeva, V. N., Vlasenko, L. V., Gibadullin, A. A., & Sadriddinov, M. I. (2019). Digitalization of organizations: Current issues, managerial challenges and socio-economic risks. *Journal of Physics: Conference Series*, 1399(3), 033038.

James, E. H., Wooten, L. P., & Dushek, K. 2011. Crisis management: Informing a new leadership research agenda. *The Academy of Management Annals*, 5(1), 455–493.

Jin, J., & Von Zedtwitz, M. (2008). Technological capability development in China's mobile phone industry. *Technovation*, 28(6), 327–334.

Klonowski, Z. J. (2004). Systemy informatyczne zarządzania przedsiębiorstwem. Wrocław: Oficyna Wydawnicza Politechniki Wrocławskiej.

Kukafka, R., Johnson, S. B., Linfante, A., & Allegrante, J. P. (2003). Grounding a new information technology implementation framework in behavioral science: A systematic analysis of the literature on IT use. *Journal of Biomedical Informatics*, 36(3), 218–227.

Lagadec, P. (2007). Crisis management in the twenty-first century: "Unthinkable" events in "inconceivable" contexts. In H. Rodr´ıguez, E. L. Quanrantelli, & R. R. Dynes (Eds.), *Handbook of Disaster Research*: 489–507. New York: Springer.

Lam, T., & Lao, T. M. (2010). Evidence on efforts to align organizational structures and business strategies. *Global Journal of Business Research*, 4(1), 71–84.

Leidner, D. E., Pan, G., & Pan, S. L. (2009). The role of IT in crisis response: Lessons from the SARS and Asian Tsunami disasters. *The Journal of Strategic Information Systems*, 18(2), 80–99.

Levin, D. Z., & Bernard H. (2008) Technology management routines that matter to technology managers. *International Journal of Technology Management* 1–2, nr 41, s. 22–37.

Liu, D. Y., Chen, S. W., & Chou, T. C. (2011). Resource fit in digital transformation: Lessons learned from the CBC Bank global e-banking project. *Management Decision*, 49(10), 1728–1742.

Longley, D., & Shain, M. (Eds.) (1985). *Macmillan dictionary of information technology*. London: Springer.

Lourel, M., Ford, M. T., Gamassou, C. E., Guéguen, N., & Hartmann, A. (2009). Negative and positive spillover between work and home: Relationship to perceived stress and job satisfaction. *Journal of Managerial Psychology*, 24(5), 438–449.

Luftman, J. (1996). *Competing in the Information Age*. New York: Oxford University Press.

Luftman, J., & Brier, T. (1999). Achieving and sustaining business-IT alignment. *California Management Review*, 42(1), 109–122.

Luftman, J., Lyytinen, K., & Zvi, T. B. (2017). Enhancing the measurement of information technology (IT) business alignment and its influence on company performance. *Journal of Information Technology*, 32(1), 26–46.

Lyytinen, K., & Hirschheim, R. (1987). Information systems failures - A survey and classification of the empirical literature. *Oxford Surveys in Information*, 4, 257–309.

Malatji, W. R., Eck, V. R., & Zuva, T. (2020). Understanding the usage, modifications, limitations and criticisms of technology acceptance model (TAM). *Advances in Science, Technology and Engineering Systems Journal*, 5(6), 113–117.

Marchand, D., Kettinger, W., & Rollins, J. (2001). *Information orientation: The link to business performance*. Oxford: Oxford University Press.

Mardiana, S., Tjakraatmadja, J. H., & Aprianingsih, A. (2015). DeLone–McLean information system success model revisited: The separation of intention to use-use and the integration of technology acceptance models. *International Journal of Economics and Financial Issues*, 5(1), 172–182.

Margherita, A., Elia, G., & Klein, M. (2021). Managing the COVID-19 emergency: A coordination framework to enhance response practices and actions. *Technological Forecasting and Social Change*, 166, 120656.

Martin, A. (2008). Digital Literacy and the "Digital". In C. Lankshear & M. Knobel (Eds.), *Digital literacies: Concepts, policies and practices*, vol. 30: 151New York: Peter Lang.

Mell, P., & Grance, T. (2021). The NIST definition of cloud computing: Recommendations of the National Institute of Standards and Technology. Special Publication 800-145, 2011.

Melville, N., Kraemer, K., & Gurbaxani, V. (2004). Information technology and organizational performance: An integrative model of IT business value. *MIS Quarterly*, 2(2), 283–322.

Milasi, S., Gonzalez-Vazquez, I., & Fernandez-Macias, E, https://joint-research-centre.ec.europa.eu/system/files/2021-06/jrc120945_policy_brief_-_covid_and_telework_final.pdf.

Miller, R. L. (2015). Rogers' innovation diffusion theory (1962, 1995). In M. N Al-Suqri & A. S. Al-Aufi (Eds.), *Information seeking behavior and technology adoption: Theories and trends*: 261–274. Oman: IGI Global.

Mimoun, E., Ben Ari, A., & Margalit, D. (2020). Psychological aspects of employment instability during the COVID-19 pandemic. *Psychological Trauma: Theory, Research, Practice, and Policy*, 12(S1), S183.

Mitroff, I. I. (1994). Crisis management and environmentalism: A natural fit. *California Management Review*, 36(2), 101–113.

Mitroff, I. I. (2005). Why some companies emerge stronger and better from a crisis: 7 essential lessons for surviving disaster. AMACOM/American Management Association.

Mitroff, I. I., & Alpaslan, M. C. (2003). Preparing for evil (vol. 81, pp. 109–115). Boston, MA, USA: Harvard Business School Pub.

Moore, G. C., & Benbasat, I. (1991). Development of an instrument to measure the perceptions of adopting an information technology innovation. *Information Systems Research*, 2(3), 192–222.

Nadikattu, R. R. (2020). Information technologies: Rebooting the world activities during COVID-19. Available at SSRN 3622733.

O'Brien, J. & Marakas, G. (2012). Introduction to Information Systems 16th Edition, Loose Leaf.

OECD. (2020). OECD interim economic assessment September 2020.

Onn, C. W., & Sorooshian, S. (2013). Mini literature analysis on information technology definition. *Information and Knowledge Management*, 3(2), 139–140.

Orlikowski, W. J., & Robey, D. (1991). Information technology and the structuring of organizations. *Information Systems Research*, 2(2), 143–169.

Otrachshenko, V., Popova, O., Nikolova, M., & Tyurina, E. (2022). COVID-19 and entrepreneurship entry and exit: Opportunity amidst adversity. *Technology in Society*, 71, 1–14.

Pan, S. L., & Zhang, S. (2020). From fighting COVID-19 pandemic to tackling sustainable development goals: An opportunity for responsible information systems research. *International Journal of Information Management*, 55, 102196.

Parameswar, N., Chaubey, A., & Dhir, S. (2021). Black swan: bibliometric analysis and development of research agenda. *Benchmarking: An International Journal*, 28(7), 2259–2279. https://doi.org/10.1108/BIJ-08-2020-0443.

Pearson, C. M., & Clair, J. A. (1998). Reframing crisis management. *Academy of Management Review*, 23(1), 59–76.

Pearson, C. M., & Mitroff, I. I. (2019). From crisis prone to crisis prepared: A framework for crisis management. In G. Mars & D. T. H. Weir (Eds.), *Risk management*: 185–196. London: Routledge.

Petter, S., DeLone, W., & McLean, E. (2008). Measuring information systems success: Models, dimensions, measures, and interrelationships. *European Journal of Information Systems*, 17(3), 236–263.

Pinch, T. (2012). The social construction of technology: A review. In R. Fox (Ed.), *Technological change*: 17–35. London: Routledge.

Pitt, L. F., Watson, R. T., & Kavan, C. B. (1995). Service quality: a measure of information systems effectiveness. *MIS Quarterly*, 173–187.

Prasada, K., Vaidya, R., & Mangipudic, M. R. (2020). Effect of occupational stress and remote working on psychological well-being of employees: an empirical analysis during covid-19 pandemic concerning information technology industry in Hyderabad. *Indian Journal of Commerce and Management Studies*, 11, 1–13.

Pun, K. F., & Hui, I. K. (2002). Integrating the safety dimension into quality management systems: a process model. *Total Quality Management*, 13(3), 373–391.

Rahman, M. H., Mutsuddi, P., Roy, S. K., Al-Amin, M., & Jannat, F. (2020). Performance efficiency evaluation of information and communication technology (ICT) application in human resource management during COVID-19 pandemic: a study on banking industry of Bangladesh. *South Asian Journal of Social Studies and Economics*, 8, 46–56.

Rajão, R., & Hayes, N. (2009). Conceptions of control and IT artefacts: An institutional account of the Amazon rainforest monitoring system. *Journal of Information Technology*, 24(4), 320–331.

Reddick, C. (2011). Information technology and emergency management: Preparedness and planning in US states. *Disasters*, 35(1), 45–61.

Reich, B., & Benbasat, I. (2000). Factors that influence the social dimension of alignment between business and information technology objectives. *MIS Quarterly*, 24(1), 81–113.

Rioveros, G. M., Reyes-Chua, E., Navigar, N. R., Solina, A. M., Lanuza, M. H., & Garcia, M. S. G. (2021). The impact of work from home set-up during the COVID-19 pandemic. *Worldwide Journal of Multidisciplinary Research and Development*, 7(8), 74–80.

Rike, B. (2003). Prepared or not... That IS the vital question. *Information Management*, 37(3), 25.

Rosenthal, U. (2003). September 11: Public administration and the study of crises and crisis management. *Administration & Society*, 35(2), 129–143.

Roux-Dufort, C. (2007). Is crisis management (only) a management of exceptions? *Journal of Contingencies and Crisis Management*, 15(2), 105–114.

Roux-Dufort, C. (2016). Delving into the roots of crises: The genealogy of surprise. In A. Schwarz, M. W. Seeger, & C. Auer (Eds.), *The handbook of international crisis communication research*: 24–33. West Sussex: Wiley.

Roztocki, N., Soja, P., & Weistroffer, H. R. (2019). The role of information and communication technologies in socioeconomic development: Towards a multidimensional framework. *Information Technology for Development*, 25(2), 171–183.

Rush, H., Bessant, J., & Hobday, M. (2007). Assessing the technological capabilities of firms: Developing a policy tool. *R&D Management*, 37(3), 221–236.

Sakurai, M., & Murayama, Y. (2019). Information technologies and disaster management–Benefits and issues. *Progress in Disaster Science*, 2, 100012.

Sapta, I., Muafi, M., & Setini, N. M. (2021). The role of technology, organizational culture, and job satisfaction in improving employee performance during the Covid-19 pandemic. *The Journal of Asian Finance, Economics, and Business*, 8(1), 495–505.

Sarosa, S., & Zowghi, D. (2003). Strategy for adopting information technology for SMEs: Experience in adopting email within an Indonesian furniture company. *Electronic Journal of Information Systems Evaluation*, 6(2), 165–176.

Savić, D. (2020). COVID-19 and work from home: Digital transformation of the workforce. *Grey Journal (TGJ)*, 16(2), 101–104.

Saxena, M., Bagga, T., & Gupta, S. (2021). "HR during covid-19 era: study on recent HR transformations through technological tools and trends". Paper Presented at the 2021 11th International Conference on Cloud Computing, Data Science and Engineering (Confluence).

Seddon, P. B. (1997). A respecification and extension of the DeLone and McLean model of IS success. *Information Systems Research*, 8(3), 240–253.

Seeger, M. W., Sellnow, T. L., & Ulmer, R. R. (2003). Communication and organizational crisis. Greenwood Publishing Group.

Shepherd, D. A., & Williams, T. (2020). Entrepreneurship responding to adversity: Equilibrating adverse events and disequilibrating persistent adversity. *Organization Theory*, 1(4), 2631787720967678.

Shrivastava, P. (1995). Industrial/environmental crises and corporate social responsibility. *Journal of Socio Economics*, 24(1), 211–227.

Solis, B., Li, C., & Szymanski, J. (2014). The 2014 state of digital transformation. *Altimeter Group*, 1(1), 1–33.

Stewart, R. A. (2008). A framework for the life cycle management of information technology projects: ProjectIT. *International Journal of Project Management*, 26(2), 203–212.

Stöhr, K., & Esveld, M. (2004). Will vaccines be available for the next influenza pandemic? *Science*, 306(5705), 2195–2196.

Strack, R., Kovács-Ondrejkovic, O., Baier, J., Antebi, P., Kavanagh, K., & Gobernado, A. L. (2021). Decoding global reskilling and career paths. Boston Consulting Group. The Network.

Sumanth, D. J. (1997). Total productivity management (TPmgt): a systemic and quantitative approach to compete in quality, price and time. CRC Press.

Sutcliffe, K. M. (1994). What executives notice: Accurate perceptions in top management teams. *Academy of Management Journal*, 37(5), 1360–1378.

Tadeusiewicz, R., Moszner, P., & Szydełko, A. (1998). Theoretical foundations of computer science. Kraków: Wydawnictwo Naukowe WSP.

Taleb, N. N. (2005). *The Black Swan: The impact of the highly improbable*. New York: Random House.

Tan, K. S., Chong, S. C., et al. (2009). Internet-based ICT adoption: Evidence from Malaysian SMEs. *Industrial Management and Data Systems*, 109(2), 224–244.

Thomas, A., & Fritz, L. (2006). Disaster relief, inc. *Harvard Business Review*, 84(11), 114–122.

Tim, Y., Pan, S. L., Ractham, P., & Kaewkitipong, L. (2017). Digitally enabled disaster response: The emergence of social media as boundary objects in a flooding disaster. *Information Systems Journal*, 27(2), 197–232.

Tom-Aba, D., Olaleye, A., Olayinka, A. T., Nguku, P., Waziri, N., Adewuyi, P., ... & Shuaib, F. (2015). Innovative technological approach to Ebola virus disease outbreak response in Nigeria using the open data kit and form hub technology. *PloS One*, 10(6), e0131000.

Tønnessen, Ø., Dhir, A., & Flåten, B. T. (2021). Digital knowledge sharing and creative performance: Work from home during the COVID-19 pandemic. *Technological Forecasting and Social Change*, 170, 120866.

Topper, B., & Lagadec, P. (2013). Fractal crises: A new path for crisis theory and management. *Journal of Contingencies and Crisis Management*, 21(1), 4–16.

Turner, B. A. (1976). Organizational and interorganizational development of disasters. *Administrative Science Quarterly*, 21(3), 378–397.

Turner, M., Kitchenham, B., Brereton, P., Charters, S., & Budgen, D. (2010). Does the technology acceptance model predict actual use? A systematic literature review. *Information and Software Technology*, 52(5), 463–479.

Tusiime, E., & Byrne, E. (2011). Information systems innovation in the humanitarian sector. *Information Technologies & International Development*, 7(4), 35.

Urbach, N., & Röglinger, M. (2019). Introduction to digitalization cases: How organizations rethink their business for the digital age. In N. Urbach & M. Röglinger (Eds.), *Digitalization cases*: 1–12. Cham: Springer.

Usher, K. (2020). Life in the pandemic: social isolation and mental health. doi: https://doi. org/10.1111/jocn, 15290.

Vahdat, S. (2021). The role of IT-based technologies on the management of human resources in the COVID-19 era. *Kybernetes*, 51(6).

Venkatesh, V., Morris, M. G., Davis, G. B., & Davis, F. D. (2003). User acceptance of information technology: Toward a unified view. *MIS Quarterly*, 27(3), 425–478.

Wade, M., & Hulland, J. (2004). The resource-based view and information systems research: Review, extension, and suggestions for future research. *MIS Quarterly*, 28(1), 107–142.

Waizenegger, L., McKenna, B., Cai, W., & Bendz, T. (2020). An affordance perspective of team collaboration and enforced working from home during COVID-19. *European Journal of Information Systems*, 29(4), 429–442.

Wang, S. (1997). Impact of information technology on organizations. *Human Systems Management*, 16(2), 83–90.

Wardman, J. K., & Mythen, G. (2016). Risk communication: against the Gods or against all odds? Problems and prospects of accounting for Black Swans. *Journal of Risk Research*, 19(10), 1220–1230.

Warner, J. (2000). What should we understand by information technology (and some hints at other issues)? In Aslib Proceedings. MCB UP Ltd.

Weick, K. E. (1988). Enacted sensemaking in crisis situations. *Journal of Management Studies*, 25(4), 305–317.

Weick, K. E., Sutcliffe, K. M., & Obstfeld, D. (1999). Organizing for high reliability: Processes of collective mindfulness. In B. M. Staw & R. I. Sutton (Eds.), *Research in Organizational Behavior*: 81–123. Greenwich, CT: JAI Press.

Weikum, G., & Vossen, G. (2001). *Transactional information systems: Theory, algorithms, and the practice of concurrency control and recovery.* San Francisco: Elsevier.

Weill, P. (2004). Don't just lead, govern: How top-performing firms govern IT. *MIS Quarterly Executive*, 3(1), 1–17.

Whisler, T. L., & Leavitt, H. J. (1958). Management in the 1980's. *Harvard Business Review*, 36(6), 41–48.

Williams, T. A., Gruber, D. A., Sutcliffe, K. M., Shepherd, D. A., & Zhao, E. Y. (2017). Organizational response to adversity: Fusing crisis management and resilience research streams. *Academy of Management Annals*, 11(2), 733–769.

Wittenberg, C. (2016). Human-CPS interaction-requirements and human– machine interaction methods for the industry 4.0. *IFAC Papers Online*, 49(19), 420–425.

World Health Organization. (2022). COVID-19 weekly epidemiological update, edition 119, 23 November 2022

Wu, H., Sun, Y., & Wolter, K. (2018). Energy-efficient decision making for mobile cloud offloading. *IEEE Transactions on Cloud Computing*, 8(2), 570–584.

Xu, J., & Lu, W. (2022). Developing a human-organization-technology fit model for information technology adoption in organizations. *Technology in Society*, 70, 102010.

Yanli, X., & Danni, L. (2021). Prospect of vocational education under the background of digital age: Analysis of European Union's "Digital Education Action Plan (2021–2027)". In *2021 International Conference on Internet, Education and Information Technology (IEIT)*: 164–167. IEEE.

Yoo, S., & Managi, S. (2020). Global mortality benefits of COVID-19 action. *Technological Forecasting and Social Change*, 160, 120231.

Yousafzai, S. Y., Foxall, G. R., & Pallister, J. G. (2007). Technology acceptance: A meta-analysis of the TAM: Part 2. *Journal of Modelling in Management*, 2(3), 281–304.

2 EDC-enabled IT adaptability model of organizational performance

2.1 IT adaptability influence on organizational performance

In new digitalized global business world, and the need for IT use on a daily basis connected with the unprecedented turbulence of the environment calls for the re-analysis of paradigms known from management sciences in order to seek for new solutions enabling organizations to maintain their continuity and thrive.

Since organizations are slowly beginning to operate in the "day after" environment, which differs significantly from the world known from before the COVID-19 pandemic and is currently an everyday challenge for contemporary entrepreneurs, which – to make matters even worse – are still either trying to avoid a crisis or experiencing various stages of it due to turbulence of environment caused by COVID-19 itself, such perspective is also important to be used as some sort of lens, through which the new models should be analyzed. Moreover, much higher level of turbulence of environment and its unpredictability causes various BSE to occur more frequently than before, which may easily force those organizations into other crises, further underlining the need for using such a lens.

Therefore, the new organizational performance model based on IT adaptability (enabled by EDC) will be introduced, showing the growing importance of IT among contemporary organizations and new characteristics of this IT which enable contemporary organizations to maximize the benefits obtained from its use.

2.2 IT adaptability

In the 21st century, organizations were forced to function under highly uncertain and rapidly changing conditions. Even before the emergence of the COVID-19 pandemic, which multiplied those characteristics, adaptation was perceived by various scholars as fundamental for the survival and success of the organization (Baard et al., 2014; Jundt, Shoss, & Huang, 2015; Marques-Quinteiro et al. 2015; Pearson & Clair, 1998; Pulakos et al., 2002).

DOI: 10.4324/9781003365044-3

Even before that, adaptability was considered by scholars as one of the four characteristics of organizations, which shape their resilience. According to Vogus and Sutcliffe (2007), adaptability, preparedness, responsiveness, and learning are drivers of organizational resilience, which is understood as "the maintenance of positive adjustment under challenging conditions such that the organization emerges from those conditions strengthened and more resourceful". Sutcliffe and Vogus (2003) underlined that organizations striving for such resilience always should seek for a presence of resources, which can be activated, combined, and recombined under new critical conditions, which may or are causing a crisis within the organization. Various authors consider adaptability as the most important driver of resilience, which allows organizations to recover from crisis caused by BSE and maintain their business continuity up until the normal conditions arise again, ensuring the possibility of the organization to "bounce back" (Koronis & Ponis, 2018). Same authors argue that it is also important for organization to be able to "bounce forward", toward business environment developed by critical conditions caused by BSE, which will arise after such BSE. Worline et al. (2002) underline that the observation shows that level of organizational resilience is influenced by the ability of the organization to develop positive adjustments and change under such critical conditions. It is also underlined by Koronis and Ponis (2018) that organizations, which are characterized by the higher level of adaptability of their vital elements (like IT, HR), are able to inspire employees' creative thinking and foster their ability for developing various creative "escape routes", which will lead the process of redesign aimed at obtaining the alignment to changing needs of the organization.

Adaptability is a characteristic which may be used to describe various elements of organization. The common understanding for all of them is placing adaptability as a characteristic, which is connected to the ability to easily change (Almutairi & Ghandour, 2021). Weibelzahl, Paramythis, A., and Masthoff (2020) describe various ways in which the word can be understood, but the main assumption behind them is the same and connects to change, even though many authors underline that the definitions available in the literature are not consistent (Andersen & Gronau, 2005).

Adaptability in the context of organization is defined as an organization's capacity to continuously change its strategy and competencies in response to environmental conditions (Albaum & Tse, 2001; Huang & Nof, 1999; Jennings & Seaman, 1994; Katsikeas, Samiee, & Theodosiou, 2006). It may be summarized into the statement that organization is adaptable when "it is to be capable of operating productivity in a competitive environment of continually and unpredictable changes" (Balve et al., 2001). Adaptability of IT should be treated as a derivative of such understanding as IT is considered here not from the perspective of computer science but management sciences, in which IT is an element of organization. Beynon-Davis (2009) defined IT as "any technology used to support information gathering, processing, distribution and use and is composed of hardware, software, data and communication technology". All elements of contemporary organizations, including such understood IT are forced to support its operation in turbulent environment – thus, they need to have the capability to realign to a changing need of the organization.

The notion of IT in organization was vastly analyzed from that point of view – offering two basic fields of research – IT-business alignment and IT dynamic capabilities. The field of research connected to IT-business alignment emerged early on in the literature and until now became a center of attention of scholars wanting to identify one characteristic, which will be crucial for ensuring stable and efficient support of IT for modern organizations (Luftman, 2003; Luftman & Kempaiah, 2007; Tworek, 2019). The field of research connected to dynamic capabilities is more recent. It is connecting IT to the need of survival in turbulent environment, business sustainability, and continuity. Heart, Maoz, and Pliskin (2010) tried to analyze the adaptability of IT in the light of the dynamic capabilities' theory (Eisenhardt & Martin, 2000; Teece, Pisano, & Shuen, 1997), staying in the context of organization and stating that it is needed for IT to be able to support any dynamic capabilities (those of itself but also those of organization as a whole). Although their work is focused on understanding the phenomenon of IT-enabled organizational adaptability, they confirmed that IT adaptability should be defined and studied in the context of organization as a whole.

However, at the center of all that research there are three characteristic/capabilities of IT – known as three AAA – which were needed in order to make sure the IT is able to provide the continuous support: agility, alignment, and adaptability. Those concepts remain important (or even became more important) in a post COVID-19 pandemic new reality (Patrucco & Kähkönen, 2021). In this reality, the following understandings should be adopted:

- Agility is understood as the ability of IT to respond to short-term changes and smooth handling of external disruptions.
- Alignment is understood as the match between organizational needs and IT capabilities.
- Adaptability is understood as the ability to adapt to occurring short-term and long-term changes.

Alignment, agility, and adaptability are often used interchangeably, which is a common mistake in the literature. They are also mixed with flexibility, which dictionary definitions connect with a broad variety of characteristics, e.g. pliability, manipulability, but also adaptability or agility (Andresen & Gronau, 2006).

However, it seems that adaptability may be a cornerstone for shaping the ability of contemporary organizations to benefit from IT, and without it, it is impossible to achieve a desired level of other characteristics concerning IT and allow organization to fully benefit from it.

IT adaptability has its origins in ISO/IEC 25010 norm, which states that 'adaptability' is 'the degree to which a product or system can effectively and efficiently be adapted for different or evolving hardware, software, or other operational or usage environments' (ISO/IEC25010:2011, 2011). Following that, Almutairi and Ghandour (2021) are stating that **IT adaptability** is "**the ability of the enterprise system to be adapted to accommodate changes in the requirements or environment of its user(s)**". Such definition seems to be in line with the general idea concerning adaptability definitions (Weibelzahl, Paramythis, & Masthoff, 2020), but offers the perspective which is generally very useful for using this term in the context of crisis occurring in organization – showing the significance of changes in the environment or users' needs as the main source of the need of adaptable IT.

IT adaptability is a very broad notion, which according to Gronau and Rohloff (2007) connects to both system-based and organization-based aspects. Many other authors are underlining the need to understand IT adaptability and its impact on the organization considering those two aspects, underlining the technical aspects and organizational aspects (naming those points of view differently, but remaining in the understanding of the need for such division) (Andresen & Gronau, 2006; Henderson & Venkatraman, 1993; Ngo-Ye & Ahsan, 2005). Such division may be also found in the studies performed by various different scholars concerning flexibility and adaptability. Han, Wang, and Naim (2017) are indicating that there is infrastructure and value-creation perspective. Infrastructure is connected with hardware, connectivity, and compatibility (Zhang, Li, & Ziegelmayer, 2009). Value-creation is connected with workflow and processes (Athey & Schmutzler, 1995).

For the purpose of this study, those two perspectives will be included, naming them: system-based perspective and organization-based perspective. System-based patterns are connected to the IT itself and its immanent qualities (resembling infrastructure perspective). However, it is important to underline that IT adaptability goes far beyond the adaptable architecture/infrastructure and need for processing the growing amount and complexity of information, even though it is sometimes misinterpreted as that in the literature (Almutairi & Ghandour, 2021). Okanga and Groenewald (2019) are analyzing the ways, in which IT can collect, assimilate, and utilize new information and determine that it is a source of improvement of the adaptive capabilities of the organization as a whole. They determined that the ability to utilize new information is a first step allowing to offer IT adaptability and may be a leverage allowing organization to benefit from IT in the broader extent (Okanga & Groenewald, 2019). However, various authors state that much more is needed to benefit from IT and turn it into an adaptive one. The "much more" can be found in the organization-based aspects of adaptability (resembling the value-creation perspective). The organization-based aspects are connected directly to the circumstances of usage of such IT in organization. It is assumed that the adaptability of IT is dependent on organization itself and specific ways, in which it is used by organization (implemented, used, and developed further). Hence, their conclusions clearly underline the need for the analysis of a mechanism, which allows organization to benefit from adaptable IT and support its proper use.

Are stating that IT adaptability is connected to some immanent qualities of IT itself. There are stating that among them there are system-based: scalability, modularity, independence, interoperability, self-organization, design, self-similarity, availability, and organization-based: structural analogy, knowledge, redundancy, customizing. It is underlined that "the degree of adaptability, which can be reached by a specific information system, is influenced by decisions referring to the deployment of the system within a business organization", which is showing the importance of organization-based aspect of IT adaptability.

However, due to the fact that IT in organization is usually a field of study, which is not uniform, in this case there are also significant research gaps concerning the definition and structuring of the nature of IT adaptability in organization. There are literature analyses concerning IT adaptability from the point of view of computer science; however, they are not fully relevant from the perspective of management sciences, for which IT is one of the elements of organization (Bieńkowska & Tworek, 2020). Therefore, the attempt should be made to present that is really understood by the term of IT adaptability in organization. It may be helpful to base that discussion on already known and well-research fields of study concerning the adaptability of other resources in organization – employees. The adaptability in the context of employees is usually presented with eight dimensions (Pulakos et al., 2002), which can be translated into dimensions of IT adaptability, what is presented in Table 2.1.

Even though various authors studied the concept of IT adaptability in the context of organization (Andresen & Gronau, 2005; Chun-Ping et al., 2007; Janssen & van der Voort, 2020; Liu and Wang, 2005; Liu et al., 2019; Reinecke, Wolter, & Van Moorsel, 2010; Xue, 2013), the coverage of this field of study is still quite poor. It should be underlined that from the point of view of this study, it is important to state that there are two points of view connected to the adaptability as the characteristic of IT (Liu et al., 2019). One point of view concerns the phase of development of new IT, in which contemporary organizations are prone to ensure its adaptability (both in case of architecture and functioning). The other point of view – the most important for the study – connects to the phases occurring after implementation of IT, in which it is used in organization. Boland and Hirschheim (1987) explained that introduction of IT into the organization is happening in six phases – startup, adoption, adaptation, acceptance, use, and integration. In this point of view on adaptability, it is crucial to underline that regardless of the phase of use of IT, it should be possible to adapt it to changing needs and such adaptation should be relatively quick if the organization wants to benefit from IT use in crisis, especially a turbulent one caused by BSE.

Table 2.1 Dimensions of IT adaptability

Dimension title (IT adaptability)	*Dimension definition*	*Source of dimension from employees perspective*	*Sources*
Support for problems solving	Solves atypical, ill-defined, and complex problems	Solving problems creatively	Hatano and Inagaki (1986); Pulakos et al. (2000); Pulakos et al. (2002)
Ability to deal with uncertain or unpredictable situations	Adjusts easily, shifts focus, and offers support for various actions	Dealing with uncertain or unpredictable work situations	Ashford (1986); Dix and Savickas (1995); Pulakos et al. (2000); Pulakos et al. (2002)
Ease of introducing new tasks, technologies, and procedures	Remains open for reconfiguration and additions of newly developed elements	Learning new tasks, technologies, and procedures	Neal and Hesketh (1999); Kinicki and Latack (1990); Pulakos et al. (2000); Pulakos et al. (2002)
Support for various means of communication	Offers various redundant communication channels	Demonstrating interpersonal adaptability	Bowen and Schneider (1988); Kozlowski et al. (1996); Pulakos et al. (2000); Pulakos et al. (2002)
Ease of infrastructure reconfiguration	Offers the possibility to adjust infrastructure to various changing factors	Demonstrating physically oriented adaptability	Pulakos et al. (2000); Pulakos et al. (2002)
Handling critical conditions	Remains available in various critical conditions	Handling work stress	Pulakos et al. (2000); Pulakos et al. (2002)
Protocols for emergencies or crisis situations	Automatically reacts to critical situations concerning its operations	Handling emergencies or crisis situations	Pulakos et al. (2000); Pulakos et al. (2002)

Source: Own work

2.2.1 IT adaptability during BSE

It is a well-known fact that ant BSE is causing the emergence of new business models that facilitate organizational agility utilizing the IT used by organization (Cao et al., 2021).

As stated before, Patrucco and Kähkönen (2021) underlined that there are three characteristic of organization and its elements, which are crucial in the post COVID-19 pandemic world from the point of view of possible BSE: agility, adaptability, and alignment. Such statement is supported by the research of other authors, who claim that there is no need to invent new capabilities to counteract the possible negative effect of BSE and it is more important to embrace the "AAA capabilities" (i.e. agility, adaptability, alignment), which are already existing in contemporary organizations, but not often treated as critical for organizational survival (Janssen & van der Voort, 2020; Lee, 2021). However, it should be considered whether all of them are truly at the same level of importance for such organizations.

Agility is considered as "dynamic context-specific, aggressively change—embracing and growth-oriented" (Andresen & Gronau, 2006). Hence, agility can be treated as the ability to rapidly respond to an external and unexpected change. However, fast and efficient behavior will be inefficient itself, when the IT does not offer the possibility to quickly realign and adapt to the changing needs of the organization. Hence, realignment will not happen without the possibility to adapt. Ngo-Ye and Ahsan (2005) are offering the realignment model of fit between changing organization needs and IT; however, once again, they are confirming that thought. Moreover, Janssen and van der Voort (2020) are proposing a comparison of agility and adaptability in the context of governance in crisis. They underline that the lead motive for deciding to underline the importance of agility is to satisfy the client; however, in case of adaptability, the main motive is to survive the crisis. The authors are stating that at the core of adaptability is the maintenance of own fit with the environment, with both subject to change. That conclusion alone allows to underline that it is a characteristic of IT, which remains extremely important from the point of view of organizational survival in crisis caused by BSE. Hence, in the context of crisis, authors once again underline that adaptability should be treated as a cornerstone also in this particular case, ensuring the possibility to obtain a desirable level of other characteristics.

The idea that IT adaptability may be a new paradigm of successful organizations, which are forced to operate in turbulent environment is not that new in the literature. Gronau and Rohloff (2007) underlined such thought already in 2007 stating that adaptable IT is crucial for any organizational transformations, which are inevitable in modern world. Nowadays, vast number of authors are underlining that IT should evolve to be able to contribute for the organizational survival allowing for the best possible response to occurring crisis (Patrucco & Kähkönen, 2021).

Considering the fact that crisis caused by BSE is at the end of an axis characterizing its turbulence, volatility, and unpredictability, the importance of IT adaptability for organization rises even higher. Based on the work of Chakravarthy (Burrell, 2021), it may be stated that the higher the level of IT adaptability, the higher level of environmental complexity can be handled by the organization.

The notion of adaptability as the primary source of survival during times of "permanent emergency" caused, among others, by BSE is well-known in the literature (Burrell, 2021; Wolff & Ladi, 2020). Wolff and Ladi (2020) are arguing that adaptive response is the most important step the organization can make during crisis caused by BSE. Gronau and Rohloff (2007) underlined that during any environmental turbulence, the lack of IT adaptability becomes a critical issue for organization, which may contribute to its lack of ability to survive.

What is also interesting from the point of view of this study, Janssen and van der Voort (2016) stated that adaptability must be supported by stability, even though they seem to be at odds. Both of them are needed in times of crisis, which was further confirmed by the second study of the same authors (Janssen & van der Voort, 2020). Adaptability implies the need to change, but only when it is followed by stability it may preserve the positive influence on organization as a whole.

It should also be stated that according to Vahdat (2021) "IT may become a boomerang for an entity if not managed effectively". He underlined that without IT adaptability, it is simply impossible to maintain proper functioning of organizations operating under conditions caused by BSE. Furthermore, other authors also confirm that IT itself is not enough to avoid the boomerang effect, it needs to be dynamic and adaptive in all situations, especially those connected with challenges coming from BSEs (Wang et al., 2021).

Therefore, it seems that IT adaptability has the potential to be a characteristic of IT use in organization, which will significantly influence the possibility of gaining benefits by organization from that use. However, it is important to identify the mechanism, which allows for such benefits to be maximized by organizations operating under conditions caused by BSE.

2.2.2 *IT adaptability, job performance, and organizational performance*

To analyze the issue of IT adaptability influence on organization, the theoretical model will be presented and discussed in parts. At the beginning, the issue of IT adaptability influence on job and organizational performance will be discussed (Figure 2.1).

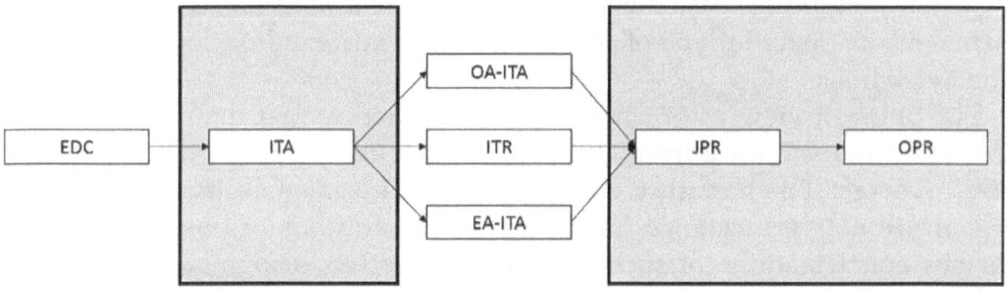

Figure 2.1 IT adaptability, job performance, organizational performance

2.2.2.1 *Organizational performance and job performance – definition*

Organizational performance is definitely a multidimensional construct "that is very often evaluated by business practitioners as sales, profits, sales change, and profit change" (Makovec, Pfajfar, & Raiakovic, 2012) and seems to be essential to the survival and success of modern organizations (Richard et al., 2009). For the purpose of this study, **organizational performance** will be understood as ***the ability to effectively implement strategies to achieve institutional objectives*** (Randeree & Al Youha, 2009). Such definition allows to underline that during crisis such objectives change and usually survival becomes the main aim of the organization for the time being, allowing for reconfiguration of resources aimed at achieving this purpose.

Job performance is also defined in various different ways (June & Mahmood, 2011). In general, it refers to property of the behavior of employees (Motowidlo & Kell, 2012; Sonnentag & Frese, 2002) and for the purpose of this study, it will be understood as ***the expected organizational value of what people do*** (Motowidlo & Kell, 2012). However, it should be underlined that job performance concerns both behavioral and outcome aspects (Sonnentag & Frese, 2002;). Sisodia and colleagues (2021) underline that employees job performance, which they are linking to "intrinsic productive capabilities of human being", plays a significant role for organizational performance. Both theoretically and practically, job performance is usually understood as the proper performance of work at the workplace and various empirical research confirms that job performance is significantly positively influencing organizational performance.

2.2.2.2 *IT adaptability influence on organizational performance through job performance*

The adaptability as a notion itself connected to the organization as a whole is known to affect the organizational performance. One of the most important strategies – adaptability – behavior model in the literature connecting adaptability to organizational performance is structuring that relation in a following way: context influences adaptability, which influences behaviors, which finally shape the organizational performance.

Such assumption is used during the development of model concerning the influence of a specific type of adaptability – IT adaptability on an organization as a whole.

The point of view of organizational performance and the role of adaptable IT in boosting it during crisis caused by BSE is having limited literature coverage. The literature on the subject of IT adaptability influence on organizational performance during normal conditions of operating shows various confirmations of such relation. It is often recognized in the literature as IS Success Model (the best-known example is the DeLone and McLean (2003) model). Moreover, most of them include three elements: IT resources, IT capabilities, and IT-business alignment (Jacks et al., 2011) and all of them have the potential to mitigate various negative effects, which may occur in the organization and negatively influence its performance. Hence, such point of view may be adopted while analyzing the role of IT adaptability in mitigating the negative effects of crisis caused by BSE on organizational performance and boosting such performance through such mechanisms.

Moreover, there is the issue of the importance of adaptable IT support as a resource, which is undoubtful and clear during crisis. The importance of IT adaptability may be supported by some literature reports. The results of the study performed by Wanasida et al. (2021) underline the importance of IT (business analytics) capabilities (determined by adaptable IT support) influence on organizational performance among organizations operating during BSE-caused crisis. They concluded that the higher the organization's business analytics capabilities (supported by adaptable IT), the more agile is the organization (which was also confirmed by Ashrafi et al., 2019) and through that – the better its performance (which was also confirmed by Darvishmotevali & Ali, 2020). It seems that it may be an example of mechanism, through which IT adaptability will positively influence organizational performance. It is also worth noting that IT adaptability allows IT to support organization in implementation of the strategy and quick decisions making process (Stank & Lackey, 1997). It is an example of another mechanism, which will improve the organizational performance through IT adaptability (Cash & Konsynski, 1985; Patterson, Grimm, & Corsi, 2003). It seems that all of them support the assumption that IT adaptability will positively influence organizational performance during crisis, especially such caused by BSE.

Moreover, IT adaptability is studied to some extent in the literature in the context of organizational sustainability – indirectly connecting to operations during crisis (Watson, Boudreau, & Chen, 2010; Zeng & Lu, 2020; Zhu et al., 2016), which connects to organizational performance, showing that the positive influence of IT adaptability on organizational performance may be indeed occurring also during crisis, especially such caused by BSE. Various authors underline that in any turbulent environment, organizational adaptability is crucial for survival and maintaining its organizational performance. In crisis caused by BSE, characterized by an extreme level of such turbulence, it is even more true. Almutairi et al. (2022) stated that adaptable IT should allow the incorporation of changes that align with evolving business goals and unforeseen disruptions. Their empirical study confirmed that assumption and allow them to conclude that organizations operating during crisis caused by BSE (specifically the COVID-19 pandemic), the IT adaptability was crucial for their survival. Marques-Quinteiro et al. (2015) are stating that "in organizational settings, as in other social systems, being able to perform adaptively is a requisite condition for sustainability", insisting that during crisis, any adaptability in organization is influencing organizational performance through employees.

The point of view of IT adaptability influence on organizational performance through job performance is much more often discussed in the literature. It is crucial to underline that adaptable IT support allows employees to perform their everyday tasks and maintain any satisfactory level of job performance, especially during crisis (Wang et al., 2020). Authors usually name two factors, which are determined by IT support: support for redesigned tasks (where IT adaptability translates into benefits for organization) and support for communication.

The need for task redesign comes directly from the characteristics of crisis caused by BSE. BSE usually cause a massive shift in the environment, causing organizations to change the way of working. The COVID-19 pandemic seems to be a good example here, as it was associated with social distancing and stay-at-home regulations, forcing employees to redesign the way they implement their tasks (Gössling & Schweiggart, 2022). Achieving that change in the way of working without the support of adaptable IT is simply impossible. Adaptable IT allows organizations to redesign the way tasks are being implemented within the organization to allow it to continue operations during crisis caused by BSE (Wanasida et al., 2021). It is crucial not only from the point of view of maintaining performance itself but also getting additional help from the government. The loans and guarantees for organizations prepared to mitigate the economic impact of BSE are usually subjected to its ability for such business redesign.

It should be stated that during crisis caused by BSE, the most critical IT support is needed by the employees. It is especially true in contemporary organizations, in which entire generation of people (dependent on IT) is becoming a main workforce (Gössling & Schweiggart, (2022) and especially in the context of controlling, which is a management method, which effectiveness is directly related to the performance of employees (Bieńkowska, 2015).

The Weisboard Six Box organization model (Griffin & Hesketh, 2003) underlined the fact that the relation between employees and technology is one of extreme importance for the organization even though in late 1970, the understanding of the need of technology use was not common yet (Weisbord, 1976). The technology boom just started, and it was already clear for the author that the relation between employees and technology, which they are forced to work with, will be a great source of strength, but also the main source of trouble for future organizations. It seems that Weisbord (1976) was correct and after the introduction of IT – specific type of technology used in organization, his statement underlining the relation between people and technology appeared to be even more justified. One of the first organization models, which included information technology, was developed by Falletta (2014) and afterwards he underlined the fact that employees and information technology are inseparably connected in contemporary organizations. Moreover, Alsahli (2018) states that IT and employees are connected to each other in a way, which should not allow to distinguish the effect of one of them on the entire organization without incorporating the effect of the other. That is true not only because employees' perception of IT is significantly influencing its value for organization but also because employees' efficiency (and their value for organization) depends on their ability to properly use IT (Rice et al., 1999). This in turn becomes particularly important in case of IT adaptability, in which the IT is frequently undergoing changes (especially during BSE-caused crisis) and the need for proper use of it becomes harder to achieve. Kabra et al. (2017) are confirming that view stating that it is important to understand the behavioral intention of employees to use IT in order to gain real benefits from that use. Moreover, any automatic IT support, which is available in the organization (including even information security tools), is not enough even without a crisis – Ifinedo (2012) suggests that missing opportunities and allowing for security incidents and breaches are usually existing in organizations due to the lack of employees' attention, and during volatile crisis caused by BSE and extreme turbulence occurring in the environment (even without the crisis within the organization itself), it becomes even more clear that IT (especially an adaptable one) will influence organizational performance through job performance of employees only when they are actually using it, not allowing it to automatically "run" in such changing circumstances.

Moreover, it should be assumed that IT adaptability role in shaping dynamic capabilities of the organization (positively influencing its performance) will also be somehow connected to its influence on employees. Moreover, it may be even assumed that the role of IT adaptability as a support for employees, who are treated as the capacity underlining the dynamic capabilities of the organization (which cannot react on its own – it reacts through the employees), is more crucial for enhancing performance of the organization as a whole than the role of IT adaptability acting as a direct enabler of organizational performance.

Therefore, based on above-mentioned discussion, it should be assumed that IT adaptability will positively influence organizational performance through job performance of employees during crisis caused by BSE.

2.2.3 Boosters of IT adaptability influence on organizational performance

As it was already established, IT adaptability has the potential to influence organizational performance through job performance of employees. However, it should be also assumed that there are three levels of organizational functioning, which have the potential to mediate the relation between IT adaptability on organizational performance as well as three levels of support. Those levels concern: institutional-level (organization as a whole), individual-level (employees as an element of that organization), and IT-level (IT as area of organization under the study). Hence, the following boosters of IT adaptability in organization will be considered:

On the institutional-level – shaping organizational strategy, policies, and culture conducive for the use and support of IT adaptability, which is achieved through managers' work and leadership.

On the individual-level – shaping employees' attitudes to foster the use and support of IT adaptability, which is achieved through their individual patterns of work and self-leadership.

On the IT-level – shaping IT characteristics in a way, which allows to maximize the possibility of use of its adaptable features, which is achieved through IT reliability.

2.2.3.1 IT reliability as a booster

2.2.3.1.1 IT RELIABILITY

The reliability of IT in organization is the notion of IT reliability emerged in the literature in the early 1980 of previous century and is defined as "a measurable property of IT solutions, useful for their control and management, identifying their quality level and pointing out potential problems (Zahedi, 1987) and directly linked to the efficiency of IT components, especially those critical to its proper operations. It is also considered as a measure of IT solutions stability over a variety of conditions" (Tworek, 2019). The model of IT reliability was developed by Tworek (2019), who proposed that the notion should be shaped by four elements connected to the use of IT in organization: system reliability, usage reliability, information reliability, and support service reliability:

System reliability is characterized mainly by the availability of the system, which is connected to its security while maintaining proper performance. The following aspects are shaping it:

- Replaceability – the ease of replacement of elements with new ones.
- Security – the ability to protect from the unauthorized access.
- Hardware stability – the rate of breakdowns of hardware.
- Hardware performance – the ability to efficiently perform computing operations.
- Availability – the ease of access and rate of unavailability for users.
- Saliency – the ease to understand the system structure.
- Compatibility – the ability to move information.

Usage reliability is an element of system reliability in the model determined mainly by efficiency of system use, its acceptance by the users, and ease of use. The following aspects are shaping it:

- Acceptance – the willingness to use the system.
- Efficiency – the level of energy needed from user to produce a desired result.
- Memorability – the level of effort needed to remember how to act in the system.

- Error proneness – the frequency of confusion within the system causing user error.
- Learnability – the level of effort needed to understand how to act in the system.
- Responsiveness – the period of time needed for system reaction to users' action.

Information reliability is characterized by ease of access to the needed information, and their accuracy while maintaining their relevance. The following aspects are shaping it:

- Accessibility – the ability of access information.
- Searchability – the ability and efficiency of searching through the information.
- Accuracy – the quality and credibility of information.
- Relevance – the ability to avoid irrelevant and overlapping information.
- Archivability – the ease of archive the information.
- Portability – the ability to move information between different environments.
- Movability – the ability to move information between disk spaces.

Support service reliability is determined by responsiveness and availability of support services for the system. The following aspects are shaping it:

- Assurance – the level of assurance that support service will perform tasks properly.
- Empathy – the ability to understand the problem.
- Quality – the ability to solve problem.
- Fail rate – the frequency of support services need caused by system fails.
- Availability – the ease of reaching support services and getting service.
- Responsiveness – the timeframe of reaching support services and getting service.

2.2.3.1.2 IT RELIABILITY AS A MEDIATOR

The importance of IT reliability for contemporary organizations has been already verified by various empirical studies performed by Tworek (2019). Moreover, it was proven to be one of three pillars shaping organizational reliability (Bieńkowska & Tworek, 2020).

The literature coverage of the role of IT reliability in sustaining organizations during crisis caused by BSE is very limited. However, among the research, which is already available, there are some conclusions which point to a statement, that IT reliability may be an important factor mitigating negative effects of crisis caused by such crisis on organizational performance

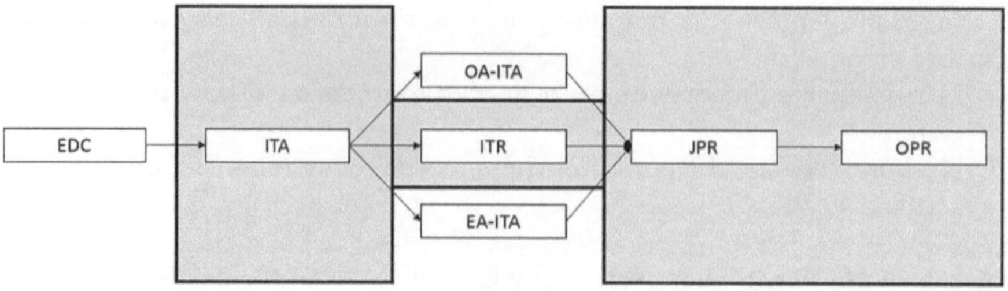

Figure 2.2 IT reliability as a mediator

(see Figure 2.2). Such mitigation occurs from two points of view: mitigation of negative effects on job performance and mitigation of negative effect on organizational performance. It seems that it is possible because IT reliability will mediate the influence of IT adaptability on organizational performance through job performance, as it will allow adaptable IT to translate into job and organizational performance also through boosting reliability – which will enable employees to be more prone to use it in crisis.

The main reason why the IT reliability should substantially influence the relation between IT adaptability and job and organizational performance during crisis is lying in the fact that they are profoundly connected with the employees' perception of their usefulness during such crisis (Martono et al., 2020; Tworek, 2021). It seems that adaptable IT is not enough if employees are not prone to use it, as they are not convinced that the adapted IT is still reliable and will produce results allowing them to fulfill their tasks with the benefit for the organization as a whole. Various authors are underlining that the cornerstone of success of use of any IT in organization lies in the fact that employees should be willingly using it to perform everyday tasks (Martono et al., 2020). Technology Acceptance Model (Davis, 1985) was a first attempt to underline the importance of acceptance for IT use. It seems that in case of IT adaptability, which is allowing IT to undergo frequent changes to align it to changing needs of the organization operating in the environment shaped by BSE, lack of acceptance will defile the possibility of organization to gain benefits from it. IT, which is not used by employees will simply not translate into higher job and organizational performance. IT reliability is connected to IT usability. In case of IT adaptability and frequent changes in the IT available for employees, its usability (especially ease of use) seems to be extremely important to allow employees to maintain its usage after such changes. In case in which IT adaptability is not backed up by usability, it is mitigating the possibility of efficient use of IT by employees, and it is impossible to achieve its positive influence on organization as a whole. Hence, IT adaptability which ensures proper reconfiguration of IT and patterns of its use will positively influence IT reliability (especially in the dimension of usability) and translate further into job and organizational performance.

The second reason why IT reliability is connected to the IT adaptability influence on organizational performance (through job performance) is the availability of such IT. IT reliability is closely connected with availability – especially as such feature is underlined as an element shaping system reliability and support services reliability, stating that their availability is a key prerequisite without it is not possible to properly use IT in organization. Such seemingly simple conclusions seem to gain importance in the critical situation, in which the availability of IT and their support services is not that apparent and accumulating efforts in order to achieve such availability in critical conditions is one of the most important tasks during crisis. In case of their unavailability, even adaptable IT will not be able to positively influence organizational performance (through job performance of employees), as it will not be operational and used by those employees. Moreover, lack of availability will prone employees to seek for other ways to fulfill their tasks, fundamentally limiting any positive influence IT may have on the organization as a whole. IT adaptability allows to boost the possibility of IT being available for employees, especially when patterns of use are reconfigured in a way which limits the possible negative effects of crisis, which may interrupt such availability.

The third reason is connected to information reliability. During BSE, the most imminent and underlined issue is connected to the uncertainty about the reliability of information flows (Lodge & Boin, 2020). In organizations, the reliability of information is also extremely important, as they are the basis on which the decisions are made, and tasks are planned and performed. Therefore, the level of reliability of information included in IT may also mediate the role of IT adaptability in shaping organizational performance, as it is directly connected to ensuring that reconfigured IT and redesign way of operating is generating reliable information, which may be used further.

In this regard, van der Lippe and Lippenyi (2020) state that reliable IT influences job performance mainly as an enabler for employees to work from various destinations (the need for which plays a huge role in tasks implementation redesign) making it available elsewhere than the main place of work. According to the authors, it is a key for increasing employees' organizational commitment and job satisfaction, because of its ability to boost their motivation. It connects to the fact that employees are aware of poorer possibility for performing their work and by contributing (sometimes more than usually) without any control they feel more independent, responsible, and committed, hence their performance is rising (Kumar & Nayar, 2021).

Hence, it seems logical to assume that IT adaptability will influence organizational performance through IT reliability and job performance.

2.2.3.2 Organizational attitudes toward IT adaptability as a booster

IT reliability is connected directly to IT itself and its characteristics. However, while discussing any IT in their context of the organization, it is crucial to

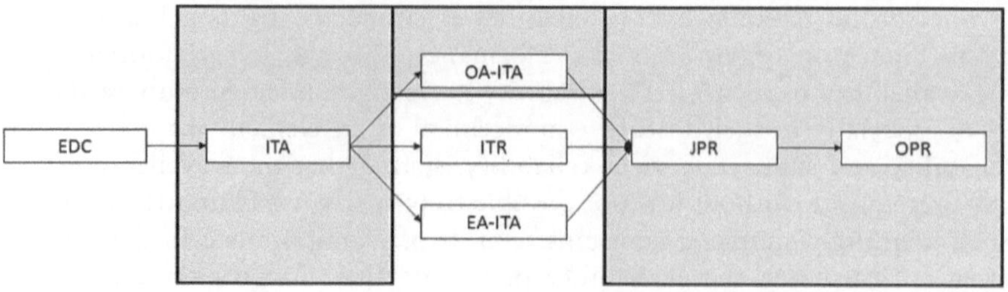

Figure 2.3 Organizational attitudes toward IT adaptability as a mediator

underline the role of such organization in establishing environment and culture prone for proper use of such IT (see Figure 2.3). IT adaptability allows IT to remain a valuable resource for the organization in crisis caused by BSE, in need for frequent and quick reconfigurations in order to mitigate arising problems. However, it is the role of organization to facilitate the use of such adaptable IT. The organization itself is unable to act, hence – such facilitation and shaping of the attitudes and culture promoting adaptability is achieved through management and their leadership.

Heart, Maoz, and Pliskin (2010) proposed three antecedents determining the organization ability to use their IT benefiting from its adaptability allowing it to match to the changing business conditions (allowing IT adaptability to translate into job and organizational performance): business governance, IT governance, and managerial capabilities (also of IT executives).

Rowold and Abrell-Vogel (2014) indicated that the most important facilitators of changes within the organization are indeed managers. The commitment of managers and their own perspective and willingness to adapt to any changes has the possibility to influence the employees. It should be considered not only from the point of view of permission to redesign the IT and patterns of its use and further down the line – using such IT for everyday tasks. It is also important to nurture such actions among employees in the form of modern leadership. It is stated in the literature that any organizations that foster behavior change and process change, especially such which is connected to most crucial organizational resources "do so to create stability, agility and resilience but, most importantly, develop a competitive advantage" (Mercedes & Burell, 2021). Therefore, the role of IT managers seems to be especially important, since they are one of the few employees in organization, who understand all three aspects connected to the ability to use adaptable IT. Business governance is a source of changing needs for them, which they need to translate into redesign of existing IT in order to ensure continuous support for the organization. IT governance is a set of tolls allowing for such redesign. And their capabilities are what makes it possible to do so. Table X is showing what is the role of managers in facilitating IT adaptability in the organization during crisis, which calls for immediate action (like those caused by BSE).

It confirms further the above-mentioned statements. As states by Heart, Maoz, and Pliskin (2010), who indicated that "the managerial capabilities of IT executives are crucial in processes that involve sensing the environment, identifying opportunities to use IT strategically, and redeploying existing or reconfigured IT resources".

Various authors vastly underline that IT cannot have a positive effect on the organization unless such organization has the governance structure which is ready to facilitate IT adaptability (Heart, Maoz, & Pliskin, 2010). Hence, it seems that organizational attitude toward IT use will be a crucial mediator allowing such use of adaptable IT to translate into higher job performance and through that – organizational performance.

Moreover, it is a well-known fact that organization culture is a factor influencing the organization ability to benefit from any adaptability within it, including IT adaptability. Closed cultures, which are not promoting the need to adapt to changes and foster adaptability, are less likely to support organizations under critical conditions.

Deverell and Olsson (2010) are proposing organizational strategic crisis adaptability typology. Even though it concerns organization as a whole, based on it a similar typology may be presented for IT adaptability. There are three groups of organizations:

1) Fully adapting organizations – they promote strategy change when BSE is occurring and both managerial and operational adaptability are in place.
2) Semi-adapting organizations – they promote strategy change when BSE is occurring, but managerial and operational adaptability are inhibited.
3) Non-adapting organizations – they promote no change in strategy and offer only operational routine adaptability.

The case studies proposed by authors clearly show that although all types of organizations where able to survive, those which offered full managerial and operational adaptability were the ones with minimal level of crisis, which occurred due to external event. Those organizations were able to translate the adaptability of its elements (including IT) into organizational performance, ensuring organizational survival and continuous operations. Deverell and Olsson (2010) are underlining that "the failure to adapt the strategy according to changes had repercussions throughout the management of the crisis" and lack of organizational support for adaptability was a factor mitigating its benefits for the organization as a whole.

Therefore, it seems that leadership will be at the center of attention in case of fostering positive organizational attitudes toward IT adaptability, allowing its use in organizations operating under crisis caused by BSE. The situational theory, which is based on a leader's ability to evaluate and create action during a specific time (Cheung-Judge & Holbeche, 2015), is especially important here, as it shows that leader can foster specific actions also in the situation of crisis occurring in the organization. Various literature covering COVID-19 as an example of BSE underline the role of managers as leaders, who emerged in the crisis and allowed organizations to survive through fostering the environment conducive to acceptance of any changes, which need to occur in it (Bajaba et al., 2021). Also, the literature concerning previous BSE is underlining the role of leadership. Boin et al. (2010) are underlining the role of leadership in case of response concerning Hurricane Katrina, stating that proper leadership is key for proper response in crisis. Hasan and Rjoub (2017) are concluding the same from the perspective of BSEs connected with war in Iraq. Hence, regardless of the source of BSE, it seems that leadership is an important mediator allowing organization to survive. It remains in line with what researchers are declaring in general – that the selection of proper leader (with proper leadership style) is a key for effective crisis management and fostering a culture which support adaptability needed in such conditions (Bowers et al., 2017). Jundt, Shoss, and Huang (2015) are underlining that leadership (especially transformational leadership) is a cornerstone for adaptive performance of employees, which allows them to function properly under the conditions caused by BSE (turbulent and unpredictable changes). Such point of view confirms that three levels of support for fostering IT adaptability in organization are indisputably linked with each other, as organization-level characteristics are creating an environment for employees, fostering characteristics conducive for IT adaptability use on that level.

2.2.3.3 Employees' attitudes toward IT adaptability as a booster

IT reliability is connected directly to IT itself and its characteristics. Organizational ability to incorporate benefitting from IT adaptability is connected to organization level of support. There is also a need to add the employees' level of support concerning benefiting from IT adaptability (see Figure 2.4). It seems that the contemporary world of organizations is seeking a way for establishing that the role of employees is as important in fostering new strategies than the role of leadership. In case of IT adaptability, it is especially clear that employees – as users – are also an important linking that is translating the benefits coming from IT support into organizational performance.

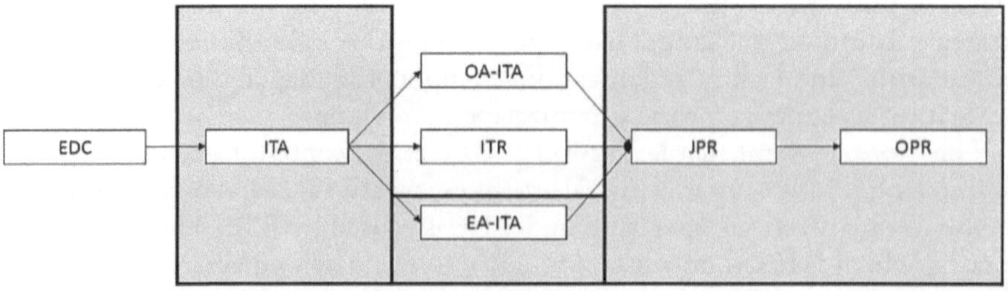

Figure 2.4 Employees' attitudes toward IT adaptability as a mediator

It should be underlined that besides the actual proper use of IT, employees have the power to facilitate its use in the organization, which is enabled by their digital competencies. Ubaidillah et al. (2020) examined the level of readiness of employees' digital competencies and determined that it is crucial in shaping any organizational response to BSEs. Such power is connected to their digital competences and ability to self-regulate – which in current literature has been placed in the field of self-leadership (Marques-Quinteiro et al., 2015). Self-leadership concerns the intentional implementation of various psychological strategies aimed at self-regulation (e.g., goal setting; performance expectancies) (Marques-Quinteiro et al., 2015; Neck & Houghton, 2006). It is a concept stating that employees are purpose driven and is proposing to set superordinate standards (i.e., reasons; motivations) that will influence goals and behaviors (Neck & Manz, 2010). Therefore, such self-leadership seems to be at the core of employees' ability to incorporate use of adaptable IT support, somehow adding its mediation potential into the perspective of IT itself (manifested in IT reliability) and organization (manifested in managers' ability to foster IT adaptability acceptance and leadership itself). Such perspective is supported by Yue (2021), who stated that leadership is not enough for organizations operating under critical conditions of BSE, especially in the new digitalized environment which is enabling employees to work from home and is giving them much more independence.

Self-leadership, similarly, to leadership, can be understood as a process through which employees influence and control their personal behavior, cognition, and motivation in the workplace (Manz, 2015; Neck & Manz, 2010). Hence, it may be a tool with the use of which they can also foster benefits gained by organization from IT adaptability. The empirical research confirming the positive relation between self-leadership employees' capabilities for adaptation in the workplace – including abilities to incorporate the adaptability of organization as a whole or its elements (like IT adaptability) is actually quite extensive (e.g., Bailey, Barber, & Justice, 2018; Hauschildt & Konradt, 2012; Marques-Quinteiro & Curral, 2012; Marques-Quinteiro et al., 2015; Pina E Cunha, Pacheco, Castanheira, & Rego, 2015; Stewart, Courtright, & Manz, 2011). That is mainly because self-leadership seems to be multiplying positive effects of EDC, allowing employees to have a greater awareness of the environment, which influences their decision-making process and in turn, positively affects their job performance and the organization as a whole (Marques-Quinteiro et al., 2015). Stewart et al. (2011) are underlining what is especially important here – that self-leadership shapes the employees' capabilities to perform tasks, which need adaptability. Hence, existing IT adaptability which addresses the changing needs of organizations operating under crisis caused by BSE (especially turbulent one) will have a better chance to be properly used by employees, who are equipped with EDC and incorporate such use because of their self-leadership in this direction. Moreover, IT adaptability will positively influence such capabilities for self-leadership, offering proper tools (from the field of IT support) to strengthen employees' adaptive performance (through their own adaptability).

The term adaptive performance is sometimes misleading and used in various aspects by scholars. Usually, the term performance in the context of employees is reserved for fulfilling organizational goals, which are behavior relevant (Campbell et al., 1993). However, some researchers consider adaptive performance "to reflect the willingness or ability to change in addition to the enactment of change behaviors" (Pulakos et al., 2000) (Jundt, Shoss, & Huang, 2015). Campbell et al. (1993) and Jundt, Shoss, and Huang (2015) are underlining that adaptive performance should be understood as behavior and distinguished from the outcomes or evaluations of the effectiveness, which means that it may attract employees to benefit from adaptability found in various places in organization (including IT) during critical conditions of BSE, which call for quick and dynamic reconfigurations of work patterns.

Hence, it seems that fostered adaptive performance may also have the potential to shape the employees ability to incorporate use of IT adaptability, which will allow it to be translated into job performance of employees (in traditionally understood terms) and then, organizational performance.

Moreover, it should be stated that employees' attitude toward adaptable IT is directly connected to their response to organizational change (Yue, 2021). Many scholars examined employees' responses to various organizational change, indicating that there are two levels of it: attitudinal and behavioral one (Oreg, Vakola, & Armenakis, 2011). Employees' commitment to any change is extensively studied in the contemporary literature, dividing it into three types: affective, normative, and continuance but in general is refers to "a force (mind-set) that binds an individual to a course of action deemed necessary for the successful implementation of a change initiative" (Meyer & Herscovitsch, 2001). From the purpose of this study, the affective commitment, which is connected to the internal desire to support changes within the organization, will be especially important in the context of fostering the environment conducive for a proper use of IT adaptability. Hence, from this point of view, the employees' attitudes also seem to be an important mediator allowing organization as a whole to gain benefits from adaptable IT.

2.2.4 IT adaptability mediated influence on organizational performance

Therefore, it seems that the extensive literature review confirms that IT adaptability has the ability to positively influence organizational performance, but that influence is much greater if it is not only direct. It seems that job performance of employees is the other important outcome variable – connected to employees as the resource, which is using IT and allowing it to have any effect at all on organization as a whole – which will be a mediator of the relation between IT adaptability and organizational performance.

It remains in line with the approach adopted by Mercedes and Burell (2021), who underline the difference between the support of managers (organizational) and employees (individual) for IT adaptability. They stated that the most important difference comes from the fact that managers should focus on amplifying the IT and its capabilities, to rapidly inject resources needed for ensuring IT support and training for that support to be efficient, while employees should focus on leveraging the IT offered by the organization, ensuring its proper use and providing feedback on that, using offered training. The second difference comes from the fact that managers should expect problems and issues and should be prepared to capture and share good practices and problems, which need to be solved asking for feedback and solicit ideas, acting as a model for continuous improvement, while employees should use learning opportunities, and share their knowledge and experience to participate in building digital competencies.

Therefore, it is assumed that there are three levels of organizational functioning, which have the potential to influence the level of benefits, which can be gained by the organizations from the adaptable IT support. Those levels concern: institutional-level (organization as a whole), individual-level (employees as an element of that organization), and IT-level (IT as area of organization under the study). The performed literature review shows that each of those level has a potential to mediate the relation between IT adaptability and organizational performance (through job performance) among organizations operating in crisis caused by BSE.

The level of organization is connected to shaping strategy, policies, and culture conducive for the use and support of IT adaptability, which is achieved through managers' work and leadership.

The level of employees is connected to shaping their attitudes to foster the use and support of IT adaptability, which is achieved through their individual patterns of work and self-leadership.

The level of IT is connected to shaping IT characteristics in a way, which allows to maximize the possibility of use of its adaptable features, which is achieved through IT reliability.

The above-mentioned discussions allow to formulate the theoretical mediation model of IT adaptability influence of organizational performance and propose a following hypothesis:

H1. IT adaptability is positively influencing organizational performance through organizational attitudes toward adaptable IT, employees' attitudes toward adaptable IT, IT reliability, and job performance.

2.2.5 EDC as an enabler of IT adaptability

Employees' Dynamic Capabilities (EDC) is a relatively new concept derived from the dynamic capabilities' theory (Bieńkowska & Tworek, 2020). The theory of dynamic capabilities seems to be an important issue connected to the organization operating during crisis, especially one caused by BSE,

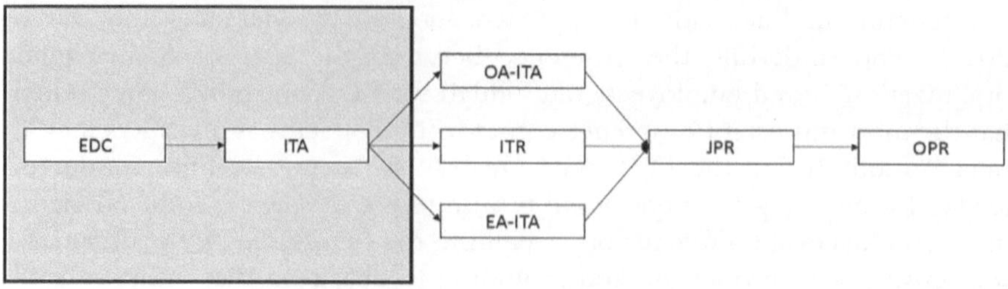

Figure 2.5 Employees' dynamic capabilities as an enabler

which calls for even quicker and more unstructured response. Various authors are performing research connected to the employees ability to adapt to the dynamic changes in the environment (e.g. Griffin & Hesketh, 2003; Jeng & Pak, 2016; Lo, 2013; Motowidlo & Kell, 2012; Pulakos et al., 2000; Sonnentag & Frese, 2002). However, they lacked clear definition of a notion connected to the dynamic capabilities of employees as a resource available in organization. **EDC**, based on the definition of dynamic capabilities of organization proposed by Teece, Pisano, and Shuen (1997, p. 516), are understood as **abilities to integrate, build, and reconfigure employees' competencies to address rapidly changing environment, which is directly influencing the performance of tasks in the workplace**. They refer to adaptability, solving current problems, but also to the long-term improvement of work processes at the job position of employees. Therefore, they are clearly an element shaping the dynamic capabilities of organization yet distinguished as one strictly connected to employees and their ability to perform their tasks. EDC is a multidimensional notion. Four dimensions of this notion are proposed (Bieńkowska & Tworek, 2020):

- "ability to be sensitive to changes in the environment (the ability to see changes, recognize opportunities and risks potentially affecting the performance of work at the workplace),
- ability to adapt to changes in the environment (the ability to undertake preventive actions, preventing the occurrence of problems in the workplace),
- ability to proactively solve problems arising in the workplace (if they occur), and include innovations in the workplace,
- ability for continuous personal development and learning".

Bieńkowska and Tworek (2020) proposed a model of job performance based on EDC, determining that EDC has the influence to positively influence job performance of employees through various work-related attitudes:

Person-job fit – a match between individual knowledge, skills, and abilities and the job requirements (Edwards, 1991; O'Reilly & Chatman, 1986).

Work motivation – conceptualized as the degree to which the employee is self-motivated to perform effectively on the job position (Hackman & Oldham, 1974).

Job satisfaction – the degree to which the employee is satisfied and happy with the job (Hackman & Oldham, 1974).

Work engagement – the ability of employees to willingly craft themselves to their work roles.

2.2.5.1 EDC INFLUENCE ON IT ADAPTABILITY

EDC is set of characteristics that help employees to quickly integrate, build, and reconfigure their competencies to meet rapidly changing environmental conditions (Bieńkowska & Tworek, 2020), hence it can be assumed that it may enable the use of IT adaptability in organization undergoing crisis caused by BSE (see Figure 2.5). It remains in line with the statement of Zeng and Lu (2020), who are underlining that IT adaptability should be supplemented by the adaptability of other elements of organization (especially employees) and other resources of the organization and only the synergy of those can significantly improve the organizational performance. Gronau and Rohloff (2007) stated that organization-based aspects of IT adaptability are connected not only to the patterns of use of such IT in organization, but most importantly to the employees using it. They stated that any dimensions connected to employees and their potential to support IT adaptability and such patterns of its use will act as an enabler of such. The research concerning the issue of adaptive performance of employees is also underlining the need for equipping employees with EDC under conditions of unpredictability (such need is multiplied under conditions caused by BSE, when the unpredictability and dynamics of environment is rising) and offering them mechanisms, which will allow them to use that EDC to enable adaptability in organization (Pulakos et al., 2000).

The relation between IT and employees is a two-sided one. IT (especially through its adaptability and reliability) is influencing employees' job performance allowing them to perform their tasks properly (which was discussed earlier). But also, employees have the ability to influence IT, especially through developing its reconfigurations and using properly its adaptability for the benefit of the organization. However, in order to do so, employees themselves must possess the needed traits, which will allow them to adapt to the changing environment and crisis occurring within the organization. That is why the EDC seems to be crucial for allowing employees to positively influence the IT in organization and its ability to positively influence the organization as a whole.

The analysis of four dimensions of EDC allows to pinpoint particular ways, in which those capabilities allow to enable the use of IT adaptability for the benefit of the entire organization. First, the ability to be sensitive to changes in the environment (the ability to see changes, recognize opportunities and risks potentially affecting the performance of work and organization as a whole) allows employees to identify the moment, in which there is a need to start developing IT reconfiguration in order to realign it to the needs of organization, which most probably will change in the near future. Any leverage the organization can get in the brief moment in which BSE already started, but the crisis has not yet occurred, may create a difference between survival of the organization and lack of it. Second, the ability to adapt to changes in the environment (the ability to undertake preventive actions, preventing the occurrence of problems in the workplace) allows employees to properly reconfigure IT in the organization to try to realign it to the changing need of the organization. Any capabilities, which allow them to properly analyze the situation, address the potential problems, and identify ways to minimize the negative effects of those problems will allow employees to more efficiently boost the IT adaptability for the benefit of the organization. Third, the ability to proactively solve problems arising in the workplace (if they occur) and include innovations in the workplace is also directly linked to the possibility to enable IT adaptability for the benefit of the organization. In those two cases (this and a previous dimension), it does not only concern the reconfiguration of IT but also reconfiguration of ways of performing tasks in order to align it to IT, which adapted to the new needs of the organization. In case of this dimension, such capability is even more important as IT usually supports in problem solving – however, it needs a correct input and development in order to fully do it. Fourth, the ability for continuous personal development and learning allows employees to foster further development of the IT adaptability, increasing its level and importance for the organization.

Some authors underline that the employees' ability to adapt to an environment rapidly changing due to the occurrence of BSE is a key to allowing organization to survive such crisis (Bieńkowska, Koszela, & Tworek, 2021). Therefore, it seems that organizations in which employees are equipped with high levels of EDC will have "a much higher capacity to adapt to changing conditions, and employees' job performance will be more likely to be ensured during crisis" (Bieńkowska, Koszela, & Tworek, 2021), also in case of its positive influence on IT adaptability.

The employees' sensitivity to changes occurring in the organization during the crisis and high adaptability to these changes have been recognized as a key factor influencing employees' job performance (Bieńkowska & Tworek, 2020; Fuller, 2010). That is because employees with a high level of EDC will consider all changes as challenges, and their approach to adapting to these changes will be highly proactive (Cullen et al., 2014; Ployhart & Bliese, 2006). By adapting to them, employees will be ready to take responsibility for the acquisition of the skills that are required by the organization facing crisis caused by Black Swan phenomena in order to work again as efficiently (Cullen et al., 2014) as possible for organization's success.

It is important to distinguish between capabilities and dynamic capabilities in order to appreciate the merits of each (Darvishmotevali & Ali, 2020).

Winter (2003) defines a capability as "a high-level routine that, together with its implementing input flows, confers upon an organization's management a set of decision options for producing significant outputs of a particular type". Dynamic capabilities, on the other hand, are geared toward effecting organizational change; they are essentially strategic in nature and, therefore, define the firm's path of evolution and development. Teece, Pisano, and Shuen (1997) define dynamic capabilities as "the ability to integrate, build, and reconfigure internal and external competences to address rapidly changing environments". Hence, by definition, dynamic capabilities involve adaptation and change, because they build, integrate, or re-configure other resources and capabilities.

Moreover, IT is gaining research attention connected to technostress and it is underlined that improper support of IT may have a negative influence on organization as a whole, confirming also from this point of view the relation: IT – employee – organization.

Hence, based on the above-mentioned discussions, the following amended hypothesis may be proposed:

H2. EDC-enabled IT adaptability is positively influencing organizational performance through organizational attitudes toward adaptable IT, employees' attitudes toward adaptable IT, IT reliability, and job performance.

2.2.6 Model in crisis

Therefore, the performed literature analysis allows to formulate hypothesis concerning the need for IT adaptability for organizations operating under critical conditions caused by BSE. Hence, the two overall hypotheses will be presented connected to two ways, in which organization can utilize IT adaptability potential:

- IT adaptability has the potential to support organization in avoiding the crisis caused by BSE-caused critical conditions.

  H3. The positive influence of EDC-enabled IT adaptability on organizational performance through organizational attitudes toward adaptable IT, employees' attitudes toward adaptable IT, IT reliability, and job performance is stronger among organizations, which have not experienced crisis even though the BSE was actively happening than among organization, which are experiencing crisis caused by BSE.
- IT adaptability has the potential to support organization in surviving the crisis caused by BSE-caused critical conditions.

  H4. EDC-enabled IT adaptability is not influencing organizational performance through organizational attitudes toward adaptable IT, employees' attitudes toward adaptable IT, IT reliability, and job performance among organizations, which have experienced the crisis caused by BSE but were not able to survive and continue their operations.

Literature

Albaum, G., & Tse, D. K. (2001). Adaptation of international marketing strategy components, competitive advantage, and firm performance: A study of Hong Kong exporters. *Journal of International Marketing*, *9*(4), 59–81.

Almutairi, A., Naeem, M. A., & Weber, G. (2022). Understanding enterprise systems adaptability: An exploratory survey. *Procedia Computer Science*, *197*, 743–750.

Almutairi, Alhanof and Ghandour, Ahmad (2021). Enterprise systems adaptability and its role to determine organisation sustainability and resilience: A systematic literature review. MENACIS2021. 4. https://aisel.aisnet.org/menacis2021/4.

Alsahli, S. F. (2018). The influence of employee's perceptions of top management support, information technology competence, technology strategy, organizational climate, and organization's nationality on information systems security, and quality success (Doctoral dissertation, Eastern Michigan University).

Andresen, K., & Gronau, N. (2005). Adaptability concepts for enterprise resource planning systems-a component framework. Americas Conference on Information Systems (AMCIS).

Andresen, K., & Gronau, N. (2006). Managing change–determining the adaptability of information systems. In European Conference on Information Systems (EMCIS).

Ashford, S. J. (1986). Feedback-seeking in individual adaptation: A resource perspective. *Academy of Management Journal*, *29*(3), 465–487.

Ashrafi, A., Ravasan, A. Z., Trkman, P., & Afshari, S. (2019). The role of business analytics capabilities in bolstering firms' agility and performance. *International Journal of Information Management*, 47, 1–15.

Athey, S., & Schmutzler, A. (1995). Product and process flexibility in an innovative environment. *The RAND Journal of Economics*, *26*(4), 557–574. https://doi.org/10.2307/ 2556006.

Baard, S. K., Rench, T. A., & Kozlowski, S. W. (2014). Performance adaptation: A theoretical integration and review. *Journal of Management*, *40*, 48–99.

Bailey, S. F., Barber, L. K., & Justice, L. M. (2018). Is self-leadership just self-regulation? Exploring construct validity with HEXACO and self-regulatory traits. *Current Psychology*, *37*, 149–161.

Bajaba, A., Bajaba, S., Algarni, M., Basahal, A., & Basahel, S. (2021). Adaptive managers as emerging leaders during the COVID-19 crisis. *Frontiers in Psychology*, *12*, 661628.

Balve, P., Wiendahl, H. H., & Westkämper, E. (2001). Order management in transformable business structures—basics and concepts. *Robotics and Computer-Integrated Manufacturing*, *17*(6), 461–468.

Beynon, D. (2009). *Business information system*. Basingstoke: Palgrave Macmillan.

Bieńkowska A. (2015). *Analiza rozwiązań i wzorce controllingu w organizacji*. Wrocław: Oficyna Wydawnicza Politechniki Wrocławskiej.

Bieńkowska, A., & Tworek, K. (2020). Job performance model based on Employees' Dynamic Capabilities (EDC). *Sustainability*, *12*(6), 2250.

Bieńkowska, A., Koszela, A., & Tworek, K. (2021). Verification of the Job Performance Model based on Employees' Dynamic Capabilities in organisations under the COVID-19 pandemic crisis. *Engineering Management in Production and Services*, *13*(3), 66–85.

Boland, R. J., & Hirschheim, R. A. (1987). Critical issues in information systems research. Wiley: Hoboken.

Bowen, D. E., & Schneider, B. (1988). Services marketing and management-implications for organizational-behavior. *Research in Organizational Behavior, 10*, 43–80.

Bowers, M. R., Hall, J. R., & Srinivasan, M. M. (2017). Organizational culture and leadership style: The missing combination for selecting the right leader for effective crisis management. *Business Horizons, 60*(4), 551–563.

Burrell, D. N. (2021). Managerial adaptability and business strategic change in age of COVID-19. *PSU Research Review* (ahead-of-print).

Campbell, J. P., McCloy, R. A., Oppler, S. H., & Sager, C. E. (1993). A theory of performance. *Personnel Selection in Organizations, 3570*, 35–70.

Cao, G., Duan, Y., Edwards, J. S., & Dwivedi, Y. K. (2021). Understanding managers' attitudes and behavioral intentions towards using artificial intelligence for organizational decision-making. *Technovation*, 106, 102312.

Cash, J. I., & Konsynski, B. R. (1985). IS redraws competitive boundaries. *Harvard Business Review, 63*(2), 134–142.

Cheung-Judge, M., & Holbeche, L. (2015). *Organization development: A practitioner's guide for OD and HR*. 2nd edition, London: Kogan Page Limited.

Chun-Ping, H., Zhen-Xiang, Z., Pei, Z., & Da-Wei, Y. (2007). Enterprise system's adaptability and its evaluation. In *2007 IEEE International Engineering Management Conference*, pp. 79–83. IEEE.

Cullen, K. L., Edwards, B. D., Casper, W., & Gue, K. R. (2014). Employees' adaptability and perceptions of change-related uncertainty: Implications for perceived organizational support, job satisfaction, and performance. *Journal of Business and Psychology, 29*(2), 269–280.

Davis, F. D. (1985). A technology acceptance model for empirically testing new end-user information systems: Theory and results (Doctoral dissertation, Massachusetts Institute of Technology).

Darvishmotevali, M., & Ali, F. (2020). Job insecurity, subjective well-being and job performance: The moderating role of psychological capital. *International Journal of Hospitality Management, 87*, 102462.

DeLone, W. H., & McLean, E. R. (2003). The DeLone and McLean model of information systems success: a ten-year update. *Journal of Management Information Systems, 19*(4), 9–30.

Deverell, E., & Olsson, E. K. (2010). Organizational culture effects on strategy and adaptability in crisis management. *Risk Management, 12*(2), 116–134.

Dix, J. E., & Savickas, M. L. (1995). Establishing a career: Developmental tasks and coping responses. *Journal of Vocational Behavior, 47*(1), 93–107.

Edwards, J. R. (1991). *Person-job fit: A conceptual integration, literature review, and methodological critique*. London: John Wiley & Sons.

Eisenhardt, K. M., & Martin, J. A. (2000) Dynamic capabilities: What are they? *Strategic Management Journal, 21*(10–11), 1105–1121.

Falletta, S. (2014). In search of HR intelligence: Evidence-based HR analytics practices in high performing companies. *People and Strategy, 36*(4), 28.

Fuller, C. (2010). Crisis and institutional change in urban governance. *Environment and Planning A, 42*(5), 1121–1137.

Gössling, S., & Schweiggart, N. (2022). Two years of COVID-19 and tourism: What we learned, and what we should have learned. *Journal of Sustainable Tourism, 30*(4), 915–931.

Griffin, B., & Hesketh, B. (2003). Adaptable behaviors for successful work and career adjustment. *Australian Journal of Psychology, 55*, 65–73.

Gronau, N., & Rohloff, M. (2007). Managing change: Business/IT alignment and adaptability of information systems. Proceedings of the Fifteenth European Conference on Information Systems, ECIS 2007, St. Gallen, Switzerland.

Hackman, J. R., & Oldham, G. R. (1974). The job diagnostic survey: An instrument for the diagnosis of jobs and the evaluation of job redesign projects. New Haven: Institution Yale University, Conn. Dept. of Administrative.

Han, J. H., Wang, Y., & Naim, M. (2017). Reconceptualization of information technology flexibility for supply chain management: An empirical study. *International Journal of Production Economics, 187*, 196–215. https://doi.org/10. 1016/j.ijpe.2017.02.018.

Hasan, A., & Rjoub, H. (2017). The role of effective leadership styles in crisis management: A study of Erbil, Iraq. *International Journal of Economics, Commerce and Management, 5*(4), 107–121.

Hatano, G., Inagaki, K., Stevenson, H., Azuma, H., & Hakuta, K. (1986). Two courses of expertise. In H. W. Stevenson, H. Azuma, & K. Hakuta (Eds.), *Child development and education in Japan*. W H Freeman/Times Books/Henry Holt & Co.

Hauschildt, K., & Konradt, U. (2012). Self-Leadership and team members' work role performance. *Journal of Managerial Psychology, 27*, 497–517.

Heart, T., Maoz, H., & Pliskin, N. (2010). From governance to adaptability: The mediating effect of IT executives' managerial capabilities. *Information Systems Management, 27*(1), 42–60.

Henderson, J., Venkatraman, N. (1993). Strategic alignment: Leveraging information technology for transforming organisations. *IBM Systems Journal, 32*, 4–16.

Huang, C.-Y., & Nof, S. Y. (1999). Enterprise agility: A view from the prism lab. *International Journal of Agile Management Systems, 1*(1), 51–60.

Ifinedo P. (2012). Understanding information systems security policy compliance: An integration of the theory of planned behavior and the protection motivation theory. *Computer Security, 31*(1), 83–95.

ISO/IEC25010:2011 (2011). Systems and software engineering – systems and software quality requirements and evaluation (square) – system and software quality models. Standard, International Organisation for Standardisation and International Electrotechnical Commission, Geneva, CH.

Jacks, T., Palvia, P., Schilhavy, R., & Wang, L. (2011). A framework for the impact of IT on organizational performance. *Business Process Management Journal*, 17(5), 846–870.

Janssen, M., & Van Der Voort, H. (2016). Adaptive governance: Towards a stable, accountable and responsive government. *Government Information Quarterly, 33*(1), 1–5.

Janssen, M., & Van der Voort, H. (2020). Agile and adaptive governance in crisis response: Lessons from the COVID-19 pandemic. *International Journal of Information Management, 55*, 102180.

Jeng, D. J. F., & Pak, A. (2016). The variable effects of dynamic capability by firm size: The interaction of innovation and marketing capabilities in competitive industries. *International Entrepreneurship and Management Journal, 12*(1), 115–130.

Jennings, D. F., & Seaman, S. L. (1994). High and low levels of organizational adaptation: An empirical analysis of strategy, structure, and performance. *Strategic Management Journal (1986–1998)*, *15*(6), 459–475.

June, S., & Mahmood, R. (2011). The relationship between role ambiguity, competency and person-job fit with the job performance of employees in the service sector SMEs in Malaysia. *Business Management Dynamics*, 1(2), 79.

Jundt, D. K., Shoss, M. K., & Huang, J. L. (2015). Individual adaptive performance in organizations: A review. *Journal of Organizational Behavior, 36*, 53–S71.

Kabra, G., Ramesh, A., Akhtar, P., & Dash, M. K. (2017). Understanding behavioural intention to use information technology: Insights from humanitarian practitioners. *Telematics and Informatics*, *34*(7), 1250–1261.

Katsikeas, C. S., Samiee, S., & Theodosiou, M. (2006). Strategy fit and performance consequences of international marketing standardization. *Strategic Management Journal*, *27*(9), 867–890.

Kinicki, A. J., & Latack, J. C. (1990). Explication of the construct of coping with involuntary job loss. *Journal of Vocational Behavior, 36*(3), 339–360.

Koronis, E., & Ponis, S. (2018). Better than before: The resilient organization in crisis mode. *Journal of Business Strategy*, 39(1).

Kozlowski, S. W., Gully, S. M., Salas, E., & Cannon-Bowers, J. A. (1996). Team leadership and development: Theory, principles, and guidelines for training leaders and teams. In M. M. Beyerlein, D. A. Johnson, & S. T. Beyerlein (Eds.), *Advances in interdisciplinary studies of work teams: Team leadership*, vol. 3: 253–291. Elsevier Science/JAI Press.

Kumar, A., & Nayar, K. R. (2021). COVID 19 and its mental health consequences. *Journal of Mental Health*, *30*(1), 1–2.

Lee, H. L. (2021). The new AAA supply chain. *Management and Business Review, 1*(1), 173–176.

Liu, X., & Wang, Q. (2005). Study on application of a quantitative evaluation approach for software architecture adaptability. In *Fifth International Conference on Quality Software (QSIC'05)*, pp. 265–272. IEEE.

Liu, Y., Esangbedo, M. O., & Bai, S. (2019). Adaptability of inter-organizational information systems based on organizational identity: Some factors of partnership for the goals. *Sustainability*, *11*(5), 1436.

Lo, F. Y. (2013). The dynamic adjustment of environment, strategy, structure, and resources on firm performance. *International Entrepreneurship and Management Journal*, *9*(2), 217–227.

Lodge, M., & Boin, A. (2020). COVID-19 as the ultimate leadership challenge: Making critical decisions without enough data. UK: British and Irish Politics and Policy, COVID-19, Featured.

Luftman, J. (2003). Assessing IT/business alignment. *Information Systems Management*, *20*(4), 9–15.

Luftman, J., & Kempaiah, R. (2007). An Update on Business-IT Alignment: "A Line" Has Been Drawn. *MIS Quarterly Executive*, *6*(3), 165–177.

Makovec Brencic, M., Pfajfar, G., & Raiakovic, M. (2012). Managing in the time of crisis: Marketing, HRM and innovations. *Journal of Business & Industrial Marketing*, *27*(6), 436–446.

Manz, C. C. (2015). Taking the self-leadership high road: Smooth surface or potholes ahead? *Academy of Management Perspectives*, *29*, 132–151.

Marques-Quinteiro, P., & Curral, L. A. (2012). Goal orientation and work role performance: Predicting adaptive and proactive work role performance through self-leadership strategies. *The Journal of Psychology, 146*, 559–577.

Marques-Quinteiro, P., Curral, L. A., & Passos, A. M. (2012). Adapting the revised self-leadership questionnaire to the Portuguese context. *Social Indicators Research, 108*, 553–564.

Marques-Quinteiro, P., Vargas, R., Eifler, N., & Curral, L. (2019). Employee adaptive performance and job satisfaction during organizational crisis: The role of self-leadership. *European Journal of Work and Organizational Psychology, 28*(1), 85–100.

Marques-Quinteiro, P., Ramos-Villagrasa, P. J., Passos, A. M., & Curral, L. (2015). Measuring adaptive performance in individuals and teams. Team Performance Management.

Martono, S., Nurkhin, A., Mukhibad, H., Anisykurlillah, I., & Wolor, C. W. (2020). Understanding the employee's intention to use information system: Technology acceptance model and information system success model approach. *The Journal of Asian Finance, Economics and Business*, 7(10), 1007–1013.

Meyer, J. P., & Herscovitch, L. (2001). Commitment in the workplace: Toward a general model. Human Resource Management Review, *11*(3), 299–326.

Mercedes, D. and Burrell, D.N. (2022), "Managerial adaptability and business strategic change in age of COVID-19", PSU Research Review, Vol. 6 No. 3, pp. 190-204.

Motowidlo, S. J., & Kell, H. J. (2012). Job performance. In N. W. Schmitt & S. High (Eds.), *Handbook of psychology*, 2nd edition: 12.New York: Wiley.

Neal, A. F., & Hesketh, B. (1999). Technology and performance. In D. Ilgen and D. Pulakos (Eds.), *The changing nature of performance: Implications for staffing, motivation and development*. San Francisco: Jossey-Bass.

Neck, C. P., & Houghton, J. D. (2006). Two decades of self-leadership theory and research: Past developments, present trends and future possibilities. *Journal of Managerial Psychology, 21*, 270–295.

Neck, C. P., & Manz, C. C. (2010). Mastering self-leadership: Empowering yourself for personal excellence. USA: Pearson.

Ngo-Ye, L., & Ahsan, M. (2005). Enterprise IT application systems agility and organizational agility. In *Americas Conference on Information Systems (AMCIS)*. https://aisel.aisnet.org/amcis2005/159.

O'Reilly, C. A., & Chatman, J. (1986). Organizational commitment and psychological attachment: The effects of compliance, identification, and internalization on prosocial behavior. *Journal of Applied Psychology, 71*(3), 492.

Okanga, B., & Groenewald, D. (2019). Optimising enterprise resource planning system to leverage a firm's absorptive and adaptive capabilities. *South African Journal of Information Management, 21*(1), 1–15.

Oreg, S., Vakola, M., & Armenakis, A. (2011). Change recipients' reactions to organizational change: A 60-year review of quantitative studies. *The Journal of Applied Behavioral Science, 47*(4), 461–452.

Patrucco, A. S., & Kähkönen, A. K. (2021). Agility, adaptability, and alignment: New capabilities for PSM in a post-pandemic world. *Journal of Purchasing and Supply Management, 27*(4), 100719.

Patterson, K. A., Grimm, C. M., & Corsi, T. M. (2003). Adopting new technologies for supply chain management. *Transportation Research Part E: Logistics and Transportation Review, 39*(2), 95–121.

Pearson, C. M., & Clair, J. A. (1998). Reframing crisis management. *Academy of Management Review, 23*(1), 59–76.

Pina E Cunha, M., Pacheco, M., Castanheira, F., & Rego, A. (2015). Reflexive work and the duality of self-leadership. *Leadership, 13*, 472–495.

Ployhart, R. E., & Bliese, P. D. (2006). Individual adaptability (I-ADAPT) theory: Conceptualizing the antecedents, consequences, and measurement of individual differences in adaptability. In Understanding adaptability: A prerequisite for effective performance within complex environments. Emerald Group Publishing Limited.

Pulakos, E. D., Arad, S., Donovan, M. A., & Plamondon, K. E. (2000). Adaptability in the workplace: Development of a taxonomy of adaptive performance. *Journal of Applied Psychology, 85*(4), 612.

Pulakos, E. D., Schmitt, N., Dorsey, D. W., Arad, S., Borman, W. C., & Hedge, J. W. (2002). Predicting adaptive performance: Further tests of a model of adaptability. *Human Performance, 15*, 299–323.

Randeree, Kasim, & Youha, Hind (2009). Strategic Management of Performance. *The International Journal of Knowledge, Culture, and Change Management: Annual Review, 9*, 123–134. 10.18848/1447-9524/CGP/v09i04/49722.

Reinecke, P., Wolter, K., & Van Moorsel, A. (2010). Evaluating the adaptivity of computing systems. *Performance Evaluation, 67*(8), 676–693.

Rice, R. E., Collins-Jarvis, L., & Zydney-Walker, S. (1999). Individual and structural influences on information technology helping relationships. *Journal of Applied Communication Research*, 27(4), 285–309.

Richard, P. D., Devinney, T. T., Yip, G., & Johnson, G. (2009). Measuring organizational performance: Towards methodological best practice. *Journal of Management*, 35(3), 718–804.

Rowold, J., & Abrell-Vogel, C. (2014). The influence of leaders' commitment to change on the effectiveness of transformational leadership in change situations – a multilevel investigation. *Journal of Organizational Change Management, 27*(6), 900–921, doi: 10.1108/JOCM-07-2012-0111.

Sisodia, G., Jadiyappa, N., & Joseph, A. (2021). The relationship between human capital and firm value: Evidence from Indian firms. *Cogent Economics & Finance, 9*(1), 1954317.

Sonnentag, S., & Frese, M. (2002). Performance concepts and performance theory. *Psychological management of individual performance, 23*(1), 3–25.

Stank, T. P., & Lackey Jr, C. W. (1997). Enhancing performance through logistical capabilities in Mexican maquiladora firms. *Journal of Business Logistics, 18*(1), 91.

Stewart, G. L., Courtright, S. H., & Manz, C. C. (2011). Self-leadership: A multilevel review. *Journal of Management, 37*, 185–222.

Sutcliffe, K. M., & Vogus, T. J. (2003). Organizing for resilience. In K. Cameron, J. E. Dutton & R.E. Quinn (Eds.), *Positive organizational scholarship*, pp. 94–110. San Francisco, CA: Berrett-Koehler.

Teece, D. J., Pisano, G., & Shuen, A. (1997). Dynamic capabilities and strategic management. *Strategic Management Journal, 18*(7): 509–533.

Teece, D. J., Pisano, G., & Shuen, A. (1997). Dynamic capabilities and strategic management. In N. Foss (Ed.), *Resources, firms, and strategies: a reader in the resource-based perspective*: 268. , Oxford: Oxford University Press.

Tworek, K. (2019). Aligning IT and Business. Cham, Switzerland: Springer International Publishing.

Tworek, K. (2021). IT reliability for ensuring performance of IT used in organizations operating under Covid-19 epidemic crisis. *Central European Business Review*, 10(1), 39–53.

Ubaidillah, E., Gunawan, I., Adha, M.A., Ariyanti, N. S., & Erviana, Y. (2020). "Students perception of technology-assisted services and readiness of employee digital competencies in covid-19 pandemic era". Paper Presented at the 6th International Conference on Education and Technology (ICET 2020).

Vahdat, S. (2021). The role of IT-based technologies on the management of human resources in the COVID-19 era. *Kybernetes*, 51(6).

Van Der Lippe, T., & Lippényi, Z. (2020). Co-workers working from home and individual and team performance. *New Technology, Work and Employment*, *35*(1), 60–79.

Vogus, T. J., & Sutcliffe, K.M. (2007). "Organizational resilience: towards a theory and research agenda". *IEEE International Conference on Systems, Man and Cybernetics Proceedings*, Montreal, 7–10 October, pp. 3418–3422.

Wanasida, A. S., Bernarto, I., Sudibjo, N., & Purwanto, A. (2021). The role of business capabilities in supporting organization agility and performance during the COVID-19 pandemic: An empirical study in Indonesia. *The Journal of Asian Finance, Economics and Business*, *8*(5), 897–911.

Wang, L., Peng, Y., Xie, Y., Chen, B. and Du, Y. (2021). A new iteration regularization method for dynamic load identification of stochastic structures. *Mechanical Systems and Signal Processing*, *156*, 107586.

Watson, R. T., Boudreau, M. C., & Chen, A. J. (2010). Information systems and environmentally sustainable development: Energy informatics and new directions for the IS community. *MIS Quarterly*, 23–38.

Weibelzahl, S., Paramythis, A., & Masthoff, J. (2020). Evaluation of adaptive systems. In *Proceedings of the 28th ACM Conference on User Modeling, Adaptation and Personalization*, pp. 394–395.

Weisbord, M. R. (1976). Organizational diagnosis: Six places to look for trouble with or without a theory. *Group & Organization Studies*, *1*(4), 430–447.

Winter S.G. (2003). Understanding dynamic capabilities. *Strategic Management Journal Special Issue*: Why Is There a Resource-Based View? Toward a Theory of Competitive Heterogeneity, *24*, 991–995.

Wolff, S., & Ladi, S. (2020). European Union responses to the Covid-19 pandemic: Adaptability in times of permanent emergency. *Journal of European Integration*, *42*(8), 1025–1040.

Worline, M. C., Dutton, J. E., Frost, P. J., Kanov, J., Lilius, J. M., & Maitlis, S. (2002). "Creating fertile soil: the organizing dynamics of resilience". Paper Presented at the annual meeting of the Academy of Management, Denver.

Xue, C. (2013). Adaptability evaluation of enterprise information systems based on object-based knowledge mesh. *Journal of Software*, *8*(5), 1237.

Yue, C. A. (2021). Navigating change in the era of COVID-19: The role of top leaders' charismatic rhetoric and employees' organizational identification. *Public Relations Review*, *47*(5), 102118.

Zahedi, F. (1987). Reliability of information systems based on the critical success factors-formulation. *Mis Quarterly*, 11(2), 187–203.

Zeng, M., & Lu, J. (2020). The impact of information technology capabilities on agri-food supply chain performance: The mediating effects of interorganizational relationships. *Journal of Enterprise Information Management*, 34(6).

Zhang, J., Li, H., & Ziegelmayer, J. L. (2009). Resource or capability? A dissection of SMEs' IT infrastructure flexibility and its relationship with IT responsiveness. *Journal of Computer Information Systems*, *50*(1), 46–53. https://doi. org/10.1080/08874417.2009.11645361.

Zhu, H., Murray, B., de Weck, O., Skelding, R., Shougarian, N., Zeidner, L., & Arnold, E. (2016). Adaptability Metric analysis for multi-mission design of manufactured products and systems. In *INCOSE International Symposium*, *26*(1), 2316–2330.

3 Empirical research and model verification

3.1 Research methodology

The proposed theoretical model was verified based on empirical research, which was funded by National Science Center in Poland by grant No. 2020/37/B/HS4/00130 titled "Development of the Job Performance model based on Employees' Dynamic Capabilities for various phases of crisis in organization".

The empirical research was conducted in two phases. Phase I was intended as pilot research, and Phase II was intended as main research. The main research tool was a questionnaire, which contained questions concerning each variable indicated in the model and various control variables. The questionnaire was prepared for top-level managers, who have a broad understanding of the way in which the organization is operating.

Phase I was aimed at verification of the quality of the research tool. The questionnaire was filled in by 25 purposefully selected top-level managers, who were acting as competent judges. Based on their input, the questionnaire was rewritten in case of several questions because of the feedback stating that there were not correctly understood. Besides that, the pilot research revealed that respondents were able to fill in the questionnaire maintaining their focus for the entire time, as the average time of questionnaire fulfillment stayed below 25 minutes.

Phase II was aimed at performing the main empirical research. It was performed in first quarter of 2021 among 1206 organizations operating in Poland, Italy, and the USA during an active wave of COVID-19 pandemic (rising number of active cases, restrictions required by most countries – social distancing, travel limitations, remote work) (Table 3.1). The COVID-19 global pandemic forced every organization to navigate into the unknown. Moreover, it caused all organizations, including those that previously treated IT support as something not worth their focus, to start relying on IT support in case of their main processes and everyday operations, including teleworking. That is why such situation was considered for the purpose of conducted empirical research as the example of BSE, which caused crisis in many organizations operating in various countries in the world and caused permanent

DOI: 10.4324/9781003365044-4

Table 3.1 The COVID-19 pandemic in Poland, Italy, and the USA

	Poland	*Italy*	*USA*
First case	March 4, 2020	January 31, 2020	January 21, 2020
Number of active cases on March 2, 2021 [during the study]	237,625	430,423	3,659,581
Daily number of deaths on March 3, 2021 [during the study]	309	348	1832
Total number of cases (March 1, 2021)	1,711,771	2,969,640	29,626,145
Month of a peak of a wave	November 2020, March 2021	November 2020, March 2021	January 2021
Vaccination starting point	December 2020	December 2020	December 2020
Currently			
Number of cases (October 9, 2022)	6,315,166	22,815,736	96,699,237
Number of cases (October 9, 2022)	6,315,166	22,815,736	96,699,237
Number of deaths (October 9, 2022)	177,756	177,519	1,087,880

Source: worldometer.com.

changes within the organizations, also those concerning the role of IT support for their survival and operations. Hence, it seems a suitable example in light of the aims of the conducted research.

Obtained results were used for statistical reasoning aimed at verification of proposed theoretical model in various stages of crisis caused by a chosen BSE. First, scale analysis was performed in order to verify whether obtained data may be a basis for next steps planned for the statistical reasoning. Second, multigroup path analysis was performed in order to verify the proposed theoretical model.

3.2 Sample selection

The empirical research was conducted using the CAWI (Computer-Assisted Web Interview) method among purposefully selected sample of organizations operating in an active wave of COVID-19 in Poland, Italy, and the USA. The sample of 1,600 organizations was randomly chosen from the purchased panel of respondents: top-level managers working in organizations, which were employing more than ten people and operating in an active wave of COVID-19, limited by the geographical scope of the activity (Poland, Italy, and the USA – countries severely hit by COVID-19 pandemic, with implemented restrictions enabling crisis within organizations). Such a method of obtaining the results from three different countries allowed to mitigate the potential common method bias. Despite the fact that the selection of organizations for the sample was not representative, it seems possible to formulate conclusions due to the diversity of the organizations included in the study and the fact that it included organizations which were not in crisis, which have not survived the crisis and those operating in various staged of crisis.

It should be noted that not all respondents provided answers to all questions. What is the most important from the perspective of this research, only 1,206 respondents answered questions related to the occurrence of the crisis in the organization induced by the COVID-19 pandemic – and only those organizations were taken into account in the main part of the statistical reasoning.

The model depicting four stages of crisis was assumed for the purpose of this empirical research, indicating following stages: prodromal stage (when the event, which will cause the crisis already happened but the full-blown crisis has not started yet), acute crisis stage (when there is sudden onset of changes, most turbulent and unpredictable), chronic crisis stage (when organization is trying to respond to crisis, which is still happening), and resolution stage (when the organization is returning to pre-crisis functioning). Hence, the obtained sample was divided into six groups:

1) organizations, which have not experienced crisis even though the BSE was actively happening (they were able to resist a potential crisis),
2) organizations experiencing crisis caused by BSE in (2a) first, (2b) second, (2c) third and (2d) fourth stage of crisis according to the abovementioned differentiation,
3) organizations, which have experienced the crisis caused by BSE but were not able to survive and continue their operations.

Table 3.2 shows the sample characteristic, showing the number of organizations operating in each country in various stages of crisis.

3.3 Variables – scales reliability and validity

To allow verification of proposed theoretical model in various states of operation (not in BSE-caused crisis, in various stages of BSE-caused crisis, not

Table 3.2 Research sample characteristic

Country	*Poland*	*USA*	*Italy*	*Total*
Not in crisis	50	9	31	90
First stage of crisis	75	68	38	181
Second stage of crisis	124	120	94	338
Third stage of crisis	121	212	44	377
Fourth stage of crisis	43	99	23	165
Not survived crisis	15	35	5	55
Total	428	543	235	1,206

Source: own work.

surviving BSE-caused crisis), the following variables were used: EDC, IT adaptability, Organizational attitudes toward adaptable IT, Employees' ability to incorporate use of adaptable IT, IT reliability, job performance, and organizational performance.

IT adaptability (ITA) was measured based on eight items connected to the dimensions of IT adaptability: support for problems solving, ability to deal with uncertain or unpredictable situations, ease of introducing new tasks, technologies, and procedures, support for various means of communication, ease of infrastructure reconfiguration, handling critical conditions, and protocols for emergencies or crisis situations. The items were measured on a 5-point Likert scale.

Organizational attitudes toward adaptable IT (OA-ITA) was measured based on three items concerning the organizational support for adaptable IT use during BSE. The items were measured on a 5-point Likert scale.

Employees' attitudes toward adaptable IT (EA-ITA) was measured based on three items concerning the employees' support for adaptable IT use during BSE. The items were measured on a 5-point Likert scale.

IT reliability (ITR) was measured based on four items connected to the dimensions of IT reliability: system reliability, information reliability, support system reliability, and usage reliability. The items were measured on a 5-point Likert scale

Employees Dynamic Capabilities (EDC) was measured based on eight items concerning four defined dimensions: sensitivity to changes in the environment, ability to adapt to changes in the environment, ability to solve problems in the workplace (including innovation in the workplace), as well as the ability of continuous personal development. The items were measured on a 5-point Likert scale.

Job Performance (JPR) was measured based on three items based on the dimensions of job performance: task proficiency, task meticulousness, and work discipline. The items were measured on a 5-point Likert scale

Organizational performance (OPR) was measured based on ten items covering all the aspects indicated in Balances Scorecard. The items were measured on a 5-point Likert scale.

To address the issue of BSE-caused crisis occurrence and its stage, the additional variable was included (C19-CS): organizations were asked whether COVID-19 pandemic caused crisis within the organization, which needed to be addressed by changing the way of their operations and if so, in which stage of crisis the organization is currently operating (prodromal, acute, chronic, or resolutions stage).

First, it was established that collected data are characterized by the normal distribution. Second, the scale analysis was performed in order to verify whether they can be used in the study and they coherently and correctly assess the phenomena, which they are aimed to assess. The scales' reliability and validity were tested using IBM SPSS software, as a first step needed for using the obtained data for further statistical reasoning. Two tests were used for that purpose: Cronbach's α and Exploratory and Confirmatory Factor Analysis (EFA and CFA). EFA and CFA were performed using IBM SPSS using the principal component rotation method. The KMO values of ITA, EDC, JPR, and OPR were all above 0.800, and the cumulative explained variance calculated in CFA (given in Table 3.3) of all variables was higher than 50%, which indicates the existence of internal structure. Moreover, CFA and fit analysis conducted using IBM SPSS AMOS confirmed that each latent variable model was above the minimal values acceptable to conduct a statistical reasoning in social sciences (c2/df < 5.000; TLI > 0.800; CFI > 0.800; GFI > 0.800; RMSEA < 0.2). The obtained results of alpha Cronbach analysis are also presented in Table 3.3. The obtained results show that almost all measurement scales are well-fitted, reliable, and coherent, as the values of Cronbach's α remain above 0.7. Besides that, the discriminant validity was tested to ensure that latent variables that represent different theoretical concepts are statistically different (the HTMT values remain below 0.65, which shows that the chosen variables may be used for path analysis). Moreover, the systematic method variance was controlled to ensure that common method bias did not occur in the chosen sample. The proposed and used scales were all previously used in various studies and the scale verification is not the main aim of this empirical research, hence the proposed set of tests seems sufficient for the indicated purpose.

Moreover, the obtained model was controlled for variables connected with the organization as a whole (based on Leavitt Diamond organization model), showing that the model is valid and stays the same for all types of conditions within the organization.

3.4 Regression analysis

First, the linear regression analysis was performed in order to verify whether proposed variables influence organizational performance in a way, which is statistically significant while including control variables, which is crucial to

Table 3.3 Variables overview

Variable	*Items*	*Alpha-Cronbach*	*Total factor load (CFA)*
ITA	8	0.913	63,073
EDC	8	0.843	47,896
OA-ITA	3	0.899	56,878
EA-ITA	3	0.854	61,345
ITR	4	0.725	55,049
JPR	4	0.753	57,759
OPR	10	0.886	49,426

Source: own work.

Table 3.4 Regression analysis results

		B	Standard error	t	p
1	(h)	1.787	0.131	13.624	0.000
	V1	0.038	0.020	1.918	0.045
	V2	0.134	0.023	5.844	0.000
	V3	0.024	0.022	1.084	0.278
	V4	0.135	0.024	5.571	0.000
	V5	0.060	0.020	2.997	0.003
	V6	0.064	0.022	2.992	0.004
	IT adaptability	0.162	0.029	2.155	0.031

Source: own work.

determine whether it is possible to carry out further statistical reasoning. The statistically significant model was obtained, which is characterized by R2 = 0.263 and F(8.1123) = 49.967, p <0.001. The statistics concerning each variable are given in Table 3.4.

The results of regression analysis clearly show that IT adaptability is a statistically significant element of the model, which includes control variables (V1–V6 concerning organizational structure, culture, technology, human capital and goals) describing elements of the organization distinguished by the Leavitt model. Hence, the statistical reasoning based on multigroup path analysis may be used in the given sample.

3.5 Multigroup path analysis

After the first step concerning scales analysis, the main statistical reasoning based on multigroup path analysis was performed using IBM SPSS AMOS software.

The statistically significant and well-fitted model was obtained through multigroup path analysis, and its baseline comparison showed that the unconstrained model characteristics were within the margins allowing to assume it for statistical reasoning. Based on them, the full assessment of the model was performed. The fit of the model was assessed with CFI (sufficient values above 0.7) and RMSEA (sufficient values below 0.2). The obtained model was statistically significant and well-fitted: Chi^2 (133) = 800.921; p = 0.001; CFI = 0.808; RMSEA = 0.064 (LO 90 = 0.060; HI 90 = 0.069). The lower RMSEA values were obtained for the models based on structural weights, intercepts, and residuals; however, CFI values for them were much smaller and hence the unconstrained one was chosen for the analysis. Hence, it can be established that comparative fit index (included the adjusted goodness of fit index) is sufficient to form conclusions based on the obtained model and the RMSEA show a very good fit in the model (calculated when CMIN has a chi square distribution under the assumption that the fitted model is correct).

3.5.1 Model for organizations operating without a crisis but under BSE conditions

The overview of the model obtained for organizations operating without crisis while BSE is occurring is presented in Table 3.5. Total and indirect effects occurring in the model are presented in Table 3.6.

Table 3.5 shows that all relations within the model are statistically significant. The relation between EDC and IT adaptability is the strongest one (e. = 0.643), which shows the importance of enabling IT adaptability with EDC. Even though the statistical significance of the relation between employees attitudes toward adaptable IT and job performance is higher in the other cases ($p = 0.029$), it still remains within an acceptable limit. There is also a statistically significant relation between job performance and organizational performance, allowing IT adaptability (enabled by EDC) to influence organizational performance.

Moreover, all the statistically significant relations within the model are characterized by estimates above 0 (positive), which means that IT adaptability (enabled by EDC) has a positive influence on organizational performance through a series of mediators.

Table 3.6 shows that the mediation occurs within the proposed model, as the indirect effects occur in case of all relations within the model. The strongest indirect effect on organizational performance occurs in case of IT adaptability, showing te = 0.159. It should be also noticed that the highest indirect effect is produced by the relation between IT adaptability and IT reliability, determining it as the strongest mediator between IT adaptability and organizational performance.

3.5.2 Model for organization operating in first stage of crisis caused by BSE

The overview of the model obtained for organizations operating in prodromal crisis stage while BSE is occurring is presented in Table 3.7. Total and indirect effects occurring in the model is presented in Table 3.8.

Table 3.5 Model overview for organizations not in crisis

			Estimate	*S.E.*	*C.R.*	*P*
ITA	<---	EDC	0.643	0.094	6.860	0.001
ITR	<---	ITA	0.662	0.076	8.706	0.001
OA-ITA	<---	ITA	0.622	0.137	4.546	0.001
EA-ITA	<---	ITA	0.424	0.120	3.538	0.001
JPR	<---	ITR	0.275	0.068	4.056	0.001
JPR	<---	OA-ITA	0.144	0.045	3.191	0.001
JPR	<---	EA-ITA	0.115	0.053	2.180	0.029
OPR	<---	JPR	0.121	0.154	0.785	0.001

Source: own work.

Table 3.6 Model effects for organizations not in crisis

Total effects

	EDC	*ITA*	*EA-ITA*	*OA-ITA*	*ITR*	*JPR*
ITA	0.643	0.000	0.000	0.000	0.000	0.000
EA-ITA	0.273	0.424	0.000	0.000	0.000	0.000
OA-ITA	0.400	0.622	0.000	0.000	0.000	0.000
ITR	0.426	0.662	0.000	0.000	0.000	0.000
JPR	0.206	0.320	0.115	0.144	0.275	0.000
OPR	0.125	0.159	0.114	0.117	0.133	0.121

Indirect effects

	EDC	*ITA*	*EA-ITA*	*OA-ITA*	*ITR*	*JPR*
ITA	0.000	0.000	0.000	0.000	0.000	0.000
EA-ITA	0.273	0.000	0.000	0.000	0.000	0.000
OA-ITA	0.400	0.000	0.000	0.000	0.000	0.000
ITR	0.426	0.000	0.000	0.000	0.000	0.000
JPR	0.206	0.320	0.000	0.000	0.000	0.000
OPR	0.125	0.159	0.114	0.117	0.133	0.000

Source: own work.

Table 3.7 Model overview for organizations in prodromal crisis stage

			Estimate	*S.E.*	*C.R.*	*P*
ITA	<---	EDC	0.343	0.083	4.150	0.001
ITR	<---	ITA	0.489	0.056	8.716	0.001
OA-ITA	<---	ITA	0.317	0.094	3.366	0.001
EA-ITA	<---	ITA	0.400	0.098	4.096	0.001
JPR	<---	ITR	0.207	0.065	3.178	0.001
JPR	<---	OA-ITA	0.200	0.044	4.522	0.001
JPR	<---	EA-ITA	0.219	0.042	5.166	0.001
OPR	<---	JPR	0.206	0.087	2.377	0.017

Source: own work.

Table 3.7 shows that all relations within the model are statistically significant. The relation between IT adaptability and IT reliability is the strongest one (e. = 0.489), which shows the importance of IT reliability as a booster of the IT adaptability influence on organizational performance. Even though the statistical significance of the relation between job performance and organizational performance is higher in the other cases ($p = 0.017$), it still remains within an acceptable limit.

Moreover, all the statistically significant relations within the model are characterized by estimates above 0 (positive), which means that IT adaptability (enabled by EDC) has a positive influence on organizational performance through a series of mediators.

Table 3.8 Model effects for organizations in prodromal crisis stage

Total effects

	EDC	*ITA*	*EA-ITA*	*OA-ITA*	*ITR*	*JPR*
ITA	0.343	0.000	0.000	0.000	0.000	0.000
EA-ITA	0.137	0.400	0.000	0.000	0.000	0.000
OA-ITA	0.109	0.317	0.000	0.000	0.000	0.000
ITR	0.168	0.489	0.000	0.000	0.000	0.000
JPR	0.086	0.252	0.219	0.200	0.207	0.000
OPR	0.018	0.052	0.045	0.041	0.042	0.206

Indirect effects

	EDC	*ITA*	*EA-ITA*	*OA-ITA*	*ITR*	*JPR*
ITA	0.000	0.000	0.000	0.000	0.000	0.000
EA-ITA	0.137	0.000	0.000	0.000	0.000	0.000
OA-ITA	0.109	0.000	0.000	0.000	0.000	0.000
ITR	0.168	0.000	0.000	0.000	0.000	0.000
JPR	0.086	0.252	0.000	0.000	0.000	0.000
OPR	0.018	0.052	0.045	0.041	0.042	0.000

Source: own work.

Table 3.8 shows that the mediation occurs within the proposed model, as the indirect effects occur in case of all relation within the model. The strongest indirect effect on organizational performance occurs, as previously, in case of IT adaptability, showing te = 0.052. It should be also noticed that the highest indirect effect is once again produced by the relation between IT adaptability and IT reliability, determining it as the strongest mediator between IT adaptability and organizational performance.

3.5.3 Model for organization operating in second stage of crisis caused by BSE

The overview of the model obtained for organizations operating in acute crisis stage while BSE is occurring is presented in Table 3.9. Total and indirect effects occurring in the model are presented in Table 3.10.

Table 3.9 shows that almost all relations within the model are statistically significant. The relation between IT adaptability and IT reliability is once again the strongest one (e. = 0.478), which shows the importance of IT reliability as a booster of the IT adaptability influence on organizational performance. What is the most important here, the relation between job performance and organizational performance is not statistically significant (p = 0.235), which shows that IT adaptability enabled by EDC has the potential to influence job performance through a series of mediators; however, it is not enough to facilitate its influence on organizational performance.

Table 3.9 Model overview for organizations in acute crisis stage

			Estimate	*S.E.*	*C.R.*	*P*
ITA	<---	EDC	0.434	0.061	7.161	0.001
ITR	<---	ITA	0.478	0.040	12.062	0.001
OA-ITA	<---	ITA	0.374	0.070	5.342	0.001
EA-ITA	<---	ITA	0.208	0.063	3.304	0.001
JPR	<---	ITR	0.300	0.047	6.391	0.001
JPR	<---	OA-ITA	0.079	0.030	2.616	0.009
JPR	<---	EA-ITA	0.156	0.034	4.564	0.001
OPR	<---	JPR	0.080	0.067	1.187	0.235

Source: own work.

Table 3.10 Model effects for organizations in acute crisis stage

Total effects						
	EDC	*ITA*	*EA-ITA*	*OA-ITA*	*ITR*	*JPR*
ITA	0.434	0.000	0.000	0.000	0.000	0.000
EA-ITA	0.090	0.208	0.000	0.000	0.000	0.000
OA-ITA	0.162	0.374	0.000	0.000	0.000	0.000
ITR	0.208	0.478	0.000	0.000	0.000	0.000
JPR	0.089	0.205	0.156	0.079	0.300	0.000
OPR	0.007	0.016	0.012	0.006	0.024	0.080
Indirect effects						
	EDC	*ITA*	*EA-ITA*	*OA-ITA*	*ITR*	*JPR*
ITA	0.000	0.000	0.000	0.000	0.000	0.000
EA-ITA	0.090	0.000	0.000	0.000	0.000	0.000
OA-ITA	0.162	0.000	0.000	0.000	0.000	0.000
ITR	0.208	0.000	0.000	0.000	0.000	0.000
JPR	0.089	0.205	0.000	0.000	0.000	0.000
OPR	0.007	0.016	0.012	0.006	0.024	0.000

Source: own work.

Moreover, all the statistically significant relations within the model are characterized by estimates above 0 (positive), which means that IT adaptability (enabled by EDC) has a positive influence on job performance through a series of mediators.

Table 3.10 shows that the mediation occurs within the proposed model, as the indirect effects occur in case of all relations within the model. The strongest indirect effect on organizational performance occurs in case of IT reliability, showing te = 0.024. It should be also noticed that the highest indirect effect is produced by the relation between IT adaptability and IT reliability, determining it as the strongest mediator between IT adaptability and organizational performance. However, the levels of effects within the model are remaining at a very small level.

3.5.4 Model for organization operating in third stage of crisis caused by BSE

The overview of the model obtained for organizations operating in chronic crisis stage while BSE is occurring is presented in Table 3.11. Total and indirect effects occurring in the model are presented in Table 3.12.

Table 3.11 shows that almost all relations within the model are statistically significant. The relation between IT adaptability and organizational attitude toward IT adaptability is the strongest one (e. = 0.579); however, it does not mean that organizational attitude toward IT adaptability is the strongest mediator in the model. That is because its relation with job performance is not statistically significant (p = 0.060). Therefore, from the point of view of the entire mediation model, the strongest and statistically significant (from the point of view of other relations) will be the relation between IT adaptability and employees' attitude toward IT adaptability (e. = 0.523). Also, the relation between job performance and organizational remains statistically significant, allowing IT adaptability to influence organizational performance through series of mediators.

Moreover, all the statistically significant relations within the model are characterized by estimates above 0 (positive), which means that IT adaptability (enabled by EDC) has a positive influence on organizational performance through a series of mediators.

Table 3.12 shows that the mediation occurs within the proposed model, as the indirect effects occur in case of all relations within the model. The strongest indirect effect on organizational performance occurs in case of IT reliability, showing te = 0.170. It should be also noticed that the highest indirect effect is produced by the relation between IT adaptability and organizational attitude toward IT adaptability, which however is not determined to be the strongest mediator within the model, as its relation with job performance

Table 3.11 Model overview for organizations in chronic crisis stage

			Estimate	*S.E.*	*C.R.*	*P*
ITA	<---	EDC	0.477	0.056	8.593	0.001
ITR	<---	ITA	0.517	0.036	14.386	0.001
OA-ITA	<---	ITA	0.579	0.060	9.643	0.001
EA-ITA	<---	ITA	0.523	0.062	8.462	0.001
JPR	<---	ITR	0.359	0.042	8.520	0.001
JPR	<---	OA-ITA	0.052	0.028	1.878	0.060
JPR	<---	EA-ITA	0.127	0.027	4.651	0.001
OPR	<---	JPR	0.473	0.057	8.291	0.001

Source: own work.

Table 3.12 Model effects for organizations in chronic crisis stage

Total effects

	EDC	*ITA*	*EA-ITA*	*OA-ITA*	*ITR*	*JPR*
ITA	0.477	0.000	0.000	0.000	0.000	0.000
EA-ITA	0.250	0.523	0.000	0.000	0.000	0.000
OA-ITA	0.277	0.579	0.000	0.000	0.000	0.000
ITR	0.247	0.517	0.000	0.000	0.000	0.000
JPR	0.135	0.282	0.127	0.052	0.359	0.000
OPR	0.064	0.133	0.060	0.025	0.170	0.473

Indirect effects

	EDC	*ITA*	*EA-ITA*	*OA-ITA*	*ITR*	*JPR*
ITA	0.000	0.000	0.000	0.000	0.000	0.000
EA-ITA	0.250	0.000	0.000	0.000	0.000	0.000
OA-ITA	0.277	0.000	0.000	0.000	0.000	0.000
ITR	0.247	0.000	0.000	0.000	0.000	0.000
JPR	0.135	0.282	0.000	0.000	0.000	0.000
OPR	0.064	0.133	0.060	0.025	0.170	0.000

Source: own work.

is not statistically significant. However, it still remained in the model creating insignificant (statistically) but quite large total effects.

3.5.5 Model for organization operating in fourth stage of crisis caused by BSE

The overview of the model obtained for organizations operating in resolution crisis stage while BSE is occurring is presented in Table 3.13. Total and indirect effects occurring in the model are presented in Table 3.14.

Table 3.13 shows that not all relations within the model are statistically significant. The strongest relation in the model occurs in case of EDC and IT adaptability (e. = 0.630); however, the relation between IT adaptability and IT reliability is almost at the same level (e. = 0.622). Considering the fact that the third strongest relation within the model occurs in case of IT reliability and job performance (e. = 0.534), it clearly shows that IT reliability is the strongest mediator between EDC-enabled IT adaptability and organizational performance. Moreover, it is the only mediator which has statistically significant relations allowing it to boost such influence. Both organizational attitude toward IT adaptability and employees' attitude toward IT adaptability have statistically insignificant relation with job performance (OA-ITA – p = 0.120; EA-ITA – p = 0.669). Therefore, from the point of view of the entire mediation model, the strongest and statistically significant mediation

Table 3.13 Model overview for organizations in resolution crisis stage

			Estimate	*S.E.*	*C.R.*	*P*
ITA	<---	EDC	0.630	0.088	7.142	0.001
ITR	<---	ITA	0.622	0.062	10.013	0.001
OA-ITA	<---	ITA	0.439	0.101	4.333	0.001
EA-ITA	<---	ITA	0.409	0.101	4.069	0.001
JPR	<---	ITR	0.534	0.071	7.551	0.001
JPR	<---	OA-ITA	0.082	0.053	1.556	0.120
JPR	<---	EA-ITA	−0.023	0.054	−0.428	0.669
OPR	<---	JPR	0.254	0.079	3.221	0.001

Source: own work.

Table 3.14 Model effects for organizations in resolution crisis stage

Total effects

	EDC	*ITA*	*EA-ITA*	*OA-ITA*	*ITR*	*JPR*
ITA	0.630	0.000	0.000	0.000	0.000	0.000
EA-ITA	0.258	0.409	0.000	0.000	0.000	0.000
OA-ITA	0.276	0.439	0.000	0.000	0.000	0.000
ITR	0.392	0.622	0.000	0.000	0.000	0.000
JPR	0.226	0.359	−0.023	0.082	0.534	0.000
OPR	0.057	0.091	−0.006	0.021	0.136	0.254

Indirect effects

	EDC	*ITA*	*EA-ITA*	*OA-ITA*	*ITR*	*JPR*
ITA	0.000	0.000	0.000	0.000	0.000	0.000
EA-ITA	0.258	0.000	0.000	0.000	0.000	0.000
OA-ITA	0.276	0.000	0.000	0.000	0.000	0.000
ITR	0.392	0.000	0.000	0.000	0.000	0.000
JPR	0.226	0.359	0.000	0.000	0.000	0.000
OPR	0.057	0.091	−0.006	0.021	0.136	0.000

Source: own work.

occurs in case of IT reliability. Also, the relation between job performance and organizational remains statistically significant, allowing IT adaptability to influence organizational performance through series of mediators.

Moreover, all the statistically significant relations within the model are characterized by estimates above 0 (positive), which means that IT adaptability (enabled by EDC) has a positive influence on organizational performance through a series of mediators.

Table 3.14 shows that the mediation occurs within the proposed model, as the indirect effects occur in case of all relations within the model. The strongest indirect effect on organizational performance occurs in case of IT reliability, showing te = 0.136. It should be also noticed that employees' attitude toward IT adaptability shows negative total and indirect effects with other variables, which however is not influencing the final model as a whole, since employees attitude toward IT adaptability is not statistically significant element of the model (its relation with job performance is statistically insignificant). The highest indirect effect is once again produced by the relation between IT adaptability and IT reliability, determining it as the strongest mediator between IT adaptability and organizational performance.

3.5.6 Model for organizations, which have not survived crisis caused by BSE

The overview of the model obtained for organizations, which did not survive crisis caused by BSE is presented in Table 3.15. Total and indirect effects occurring in the model are presented in Table 3.16.

Table 3.15 shows that almost all relations within the model are not statistically significant. One of the two statistically significant relation occurs between EDC and IT adaptability (e. = 0.484), showing the potential of EDC to enable IT adaptability. The second one of those two occurs in case of IT adaptability and IT reliability (e. = 0.329), showing that IT adaptability has the potential to positively influence IT reliability. However, all the other relations occurring within the model were proven to not be statistically significant, which shows the inability of IT adaptability to influence not only organizational performance, but even job performance of employees.

Hence, due to lack of statistical significance, IT adaptability (enabled by EDC) has no influence on organizational performance through a series of mediators.

Table 3.16 shows that the mediation does not occur within the proposed model, as the indirect effects do not occur in case of all relations within the model or even if they do – the relations are not statistically significant. Due to the results shown in Table 3.15, it is not valid to analyze the results obtained from the path analysis effects, as they are either small or insignificant. Hence, IT adaptability seems to be indeed enabled by EDC (te = 0.484), but the

Table 3.15 Model overview for organizations, which did not survive crisis

			Estimate	*S.E.*	*C.R.*	*P*
ITA	<---	EDC	0.484	0.185	2.615	0.009
ITR	<---	ITA	0.329	0.148	2.217	0.027
OA-ITA	<---	ITA	0.211	0.216	0.976	0.329
EA-ITA	<---	ITA	0.068	0.223	0.306	0.760
JPR	<---	ITR	0.287	0.134	2.140	0.032
JPR	<---	OA-ITA	0.133	0.093	1.420	0.156
JPR	<---	EA-ITA	0.000	0.092	−0.001	0.999
OPR	<---	JPR	0.193	0.156	1.237	0.216

Source: own work.

Table 3.16 Model effects for organizations, which did not survive crisis

Total effects						
	EDC	*ITA*	*EA-ITA*	*OA-ITA*	*ITR*	*JPR*
ITA	0.484	0.000	0.000	0.000	0.000	0.000
EA-ITA	0.033	0.068	0.000	0.000	0.000	0.000
OA-ITA	0.102	0.211	0.000	0.000	0.000	0.000
ITR	0.159	0.329	0.000	0.000	0.000	0.000
JPR	0.059	0.122	0.000	0.133	0.287	0.000
OPR	0.011	0.024	0.000	0.026	0.056	0.193
Indirect effects						
	EDC	*ITA*	*EA-ITA*	*OA-ITA*	*ITR*	*JPR*
ITA	0.000	0.000	0.000	0.000	0.000	0.000
EA-ITA	0.033	0.000	0.000	0.000	0.000	0.000
OA-ITA	0.102	0.000	0.000	0.000	0.000	0.000
ITR	0.159	0.000	0.000	0.000	0.000	0.000
JPR	0.059	0.122	0.000	0.000	0.000	0.000
OPR	0.011	0.024	0.000	0.026	0.056	0.000

Source: own work.

model does not allow IT adaptability to influence organizational performance, either directly or not.

3.6 Research results description

The analysis of obtained results allow to form a set of conclusions based on statistical reasoning, which are crucial in the process of the verification of proposed hypotheses.

First, the fact that statistically significant model was obtained for operating organizations (excluding those, which are no longer operating – has not survived the crisis), showing that all assumed relations within the model are statistically significant, allows to accept the hypothesis H1 stating that IT adaptability is positively influencing organizational performance through organizational attitudes toward adaptable IT, employees' attitudes toward adaptable IT, IT reliability, and job performance. The results show that the assumed relations, in which IT adaptability has the ability to influence organizational performance through various variables are existing among organizations operating in crisis and those operating not in crisis, but under the critical circumstances caused by BSE. However, it must be underlined that the empirical studies are based on COVID-19 as an example of BSE.

Second, the statistically significant model includes EDC as the first independent variable in the path model, hence it confirms that indeed EDC has the potential to positively influence IT adaptability within the proposed theoretical model. Therefore, it allows to accept the hypothesis H2 depicting the entire proposed model, stating that EDC-enabled IT adaptability is positively influencing organizational performance through organizational attitudes toward adaptable IT, employees' attitudes toward adaptable IT, IT reliability, and job performance. Such statement, in turn, confirms the main assumption of the study, depicted by the theoretical model.

Moreover, the analysis of total effects occurring within each group of organizations shows significant differences among them. The first analysis concerned the differences between three groups of organizations:

1) organizations, which have not experienced crisis even though the BSE was actively happening (they were able to resist a potential crisis),
2) organizations experiencing crisis caused by BSE in various stages of crisis,
3) organizations, which have experienced the crisis caused by BSE but were not able to survive and continue their operations.

First, it should be stated that organizations, which have not experienced the crisis due to BSE, are characterized by much higher total effects of IT adaptability influence on organizational performance (te = 0.159) than organizations, which have experienced crisis (in various stages of such crisis). It should also be underlined that other variables within the model, including EDC (an enabler of IT adaptability) are also characterized by higher total effects of their influence on organizational performance (shown in Tables 3.5–3.16). Hence, the obtained results allow to accept hypothesis H3 stating that the positive influence of EDC-enabled IT adaptability on organizational performance through organizational attitudes toward adaptable IT, employees' ability to incorporate use of adaptable IT, IT reliability, and job performance is stronger among organizations, which have not experienced crisis even though the BSE was actively happening than among organization, which are experiencing crisis caused by BSE.

Second, the results also clearly show that the model obtained for group of organizations, which have not survived the crisis does not contain the statistically significant relations among proposed set of variables, with the exception of the relation between EDC and IT adaptability. Hence, it shows that even though EDC still positively influences IT adaptability, it does not translate into organizational performance. Therefore, those results allow us to accept the hypothesis H4 stating that EDC-enabled IT adaptability is not influencing organizational performance through organizational attitudes toward adaptable IT, employees' attitudes toward adaptable IT, IT reliability, and job performance among organizations, which have experienced the crisis caused by BSE but were not able to survive and continue their operations.

The detailed conclusions (both theoretical and practical) coming from the obtained results will be discussed in the next chapter.

Appendix A

Questionnaire items

EDC

1. Employees quickly notice and successfully recognize in the environment (both inside and outside of the organization) opportunities and threats (including early warning signals) that can affect the work they do.
   Strongly agree; Agree; Neither agree nor disagree; Disagree; Strongly disagree
2. Employees adapt effectively to the opportunities and threats appearing in the environment (both inside and outside the organization).
   Strongly agree; Agree; Neither agree nor disagree; Disagree; Strongly disagree
3. Employees undertake preventive actions that will enable them to carry out the tasks entrusted to them despite changes in the environment.
   Strongly agree; Agree; Neither agree nor disagree; Disagree; Strongly disagree
4. Employees quickly notice and successfully recognize problems appearing at the workplace.
   Strongly agree; Agree; Neither agree nor disagree; Disagree; Strongly disagree
5. Employees quickly solve appearing problems, they do it on their own or seek support (within the scope of knowledge and information) that allow them to perform assigned tasks.
   Strongly agree; Agree; Neither agree nor disagree; Disagree; Strongly disagree
6. Employees generate innovative ideas and original solutions to problems.
   Strongly agree; Agree; Neither agree nor disagree; Disagree; Strongly disagree
7. Employees constantly develop their competences and raise qualifications.
   Strongly agree; Agree; Neither agree nor disagree; Disagree; Strongly disagree
8. Employees develop themselves through their work.
   Strongly agree; Agree; Neither agree nor disagree; Disagree; Strongly disagree

IT adaptability

1. IT provides efficient and adaptable support for employees during the crisis.
   Strongly agree; Agree; Neither agree nor disagree; Disagree; Strongly disagree

2. The set of information systems used by employees has changed after the beginning of the crisis and the current organization is using a much wider set of information systems than before the crisis.
   Strongly agree; Agree; Neither agree nor disagree; Disagree; Strongly disagree
3. IT provides support for problems solving.
   Strongly agree; Agree; Neither agree nor disagree; Disagree; Strongly disagree
4. IT provides the organization the ability to deal with uncertain or unpredictable situations.
   Strongly agree; Agree; Neither agree nor disagree; Disagree; Strongly disagree
5. IT is characterized by ease of introducing new tasks, technologies, and procedures.
   Strongly agree; Agree; Neither agree nor disagree; Disagree; Strongly disagree
6. IT is characterized by ease of infrastructure reconfiguration.
   Strongly agree; Agree; Neither agree nor disagree; Disagree; Strongly disagree
7. IT provides support for various means of communication.
   Strongly agree; Agree; Neither agree nor disagree; Disagree; Strongly disagree
8. IT support handling critical conditions and protocols for emergencies or crisis situations.
   Strongly agree; Agree; Neither agree nor disagree; Disagree; Strongly disagree

Employees support toward IT adaptability

1. Employees think that implementation of changes in IT caused by COVID-19 in the organization will have a positive effect on how they accomplish work.
   Strongly agree; Agree; Neither agree nor disagree; Disagree; Strongly disagree
2. Employees are willing to actively support changes in IT support for the organization caused by COVID-19.
   Strongly agree; Agree; Neither agree nor disagree; Disagree; Strongly disagree
3. Employees are willing to use the IT, which is adapted to accommodate changes caused by COVID-19 in the organization.
   Strongly agree; Agree; Neither agree nor disagree; Disagree; Strongly disagree

Organizational support toward IT adaptability

1. Organization is shaping its policies to support implementation and use of changes in IT caused by COVID-19.
   Strongly agree; Agree; Neither agree nor disagree; Disagree; Strongly disagree
2. Managers are actively fostering introduction of changes in IT support for the organization caused by COVID-19.
   Strongly agree; Agree; Neither agree nor disagree; Disagree; Strongly disagree
3. Managers are willing to foster use the IT, which is adapted to accommodate changes caused by COVID-19 in the organization.
   Strongly agree; Agree; Neither agree nor disagree; Disagree; Strongly disagree

IT reliability

1. Information systems, which are used in the company to perform tasks are reliable (they are characterized by high availability, stability, and security).
   Strongly agree; Agree; Neither agree nor disagree; Disagree; Strongly disagree
2. Usability of those information systems is high (they are efficient, accepted, and easy to use).
   Strongly agree; Agree; Neither agree nor disagree; Disagree; Strongly disagree
3. Information included in those information systems are reliable (they are accurate, relevant, and easily accessible).
   Strongly agree; Agree; Neither agree nor disagree; Disagree; Strongly disagree
4. Support services for those information systems are reliable (they are available and responsive).
   Strongly agree; Agree; Neither agree nor disagree; Disagree; Strongly disagree

Job performance

1. Please assess the work of employees in the context of job quality:
   very poor / poor / fair / good / very good
2. Please assess the work of employees in the context of job efficiency:
   very poor / poor / fair / good / very good
3. Please assess the work of employees in the context of punctuality:
   very poor / poor / fair / good / very good
4. Please assess the work of employees in the context of effectiveness of achieving goals at the workplace:
   very poor / poor / fair / good / very good

Organizational performance

1. The overall financial situation of the organization compared to main competitors is:
   Much better than competitors; Better than competitors; As competitors; Worse than competitors; Much worse than competitors
2. The job performance compared to main competitors is:
   Much better than competitors; Better than competitors; As competitors; Worse than competitors; Much worse than competitors
3. The quality of products or services (reliability, diligence) compared to main competitors is:
   Much better than competitors; Better than competitors; As competitors; Worse than competitors; Much worse than competitors
4. The innovativeness of products or services compared to main competitors is:
   Much better than competitors; Better than competitors; As competitors; Worse than competitors; Much worse than competitors
5. The modernity of applied technological solutions compared to main competitors is:
   Much better than competitors; Better than competitors; As competitors; Worse than competitors; Much worse than competitors
6. The efficiency of the organization management compared to main competitors is:
   Much better than competitors; Better than competitors; As competitors; Worse than competitors; Much worse than competitors
7. The reliability of business processes compared to main competitors is:
   Much better than competitors; Better than competitors; As competitors; Worse than competitors; Much worse than competitors
8. The market share compared to main competitors is:
   Much better than competitors; Better than competitors; As competitors; Worse than competitors; Much worse than competitors
9. The customers satisfaction compared to main competitors is:
   Much better than competitors; Better than competitors; As competitors; Worse than competitors; Much worse than competitors
10. The employees' satisfaction compared to main competitors is:
    Much better than competitors; Better than competitors; As competitors; Worse than competitors; Much worse than competitors

Crisis

1. In which phase of crisis is currently the organization?
   a. The organization is not in crisis.
   b. The organization detected signals, which inform that a crisis may occur.
   c. The organization is currently implementing preparations to prevent the predicted crisis.

   d. The organization is currently implementing a containment plan and damage limitation measures to contain the crisis.
   e. The organization is recovering from the crisis and its parameters are growing.
   f. The organization is failing to recover from the crisis and its parameters are declining even though all measures were implemented to contain the crisis.
   g. The organization is currently learning from the recent crisis.

Control questions

1. What is the size of employment in the organization?
   a. Less than 10 people
   b. 10 and more people, but less than 50 people
   c. 50 and more people, but less than 250
   d. 250 and more
2. In what country the organization operates?
   a. Poland
   b. USA
   c. Italy
3. What is the primary source of revenue for the organization?
   a. Production
   b. Trade
   c. Service
4. What is the type of the organization?
   a. Local company
   b. Branch of a global company
5. How long does the organization operate?
   a. Less than a year
   b. More than a year but less than 5 years
   c. More than 5 years but less than 20 years
   d. More than 20 years

Leavitt's control questions

1. Organization's environment is constantly changing.
   Strongly agree; Agree; Neither agree nor disagree; Disagree; Strongly disagree
2. Changes in the organization's environment are unpredictable.
   Strongly agree; Agree; Neither agree nor disagree; Disagree; Strongly disagree
3. The organization offers a lot of different products or services.
   Strongly agree; Agree; Neither agree nor disagree; Disagree; Strongly disagree

4. Manufacturing process is routine, tasks are repeatable.
   Strongly agree; Agree; Neither agree nor disagree; Disagree; Strongly disagree
5. Organizational culture is strong and Employees are sharing it willingly.
   Strongly agree; Agree; Neither agree nor disagree; Disagree; Strongly disagree
6. Most of employees have a higher degree of education.
   Strongly agree; Agree; Neither agree nor disagree; Disagree; Strongly disagree

COVID-19 control questions

1. COVID-19 is critical for the long-term success of the organization.
   Strongly agree; Agree; Neither agree nor disagree; Disagree; Strongly disagree
2. COVID-19 is a priority to the organization.
   Strongly agree; Agree; Neither agree nor disagree; Disagree; Strongly disagree
3. COVID-19 is an important event for the organization.
   Strongly agree; Agree; Neither agree nor disagree; Disagree; Strongly disagree
4. COVID-19 disrupts the organization's ability to get its work done.
   Strongly agree; Agree; Neither agree nor disagree; Disagree; Strongly disagree
5. COVID-19 causes the organization to stop and think about how to respond.
   Strongly agree; Agree; Neither agree nor disagree; Disagree; Strongly disagree
6. COVID-19 required the organization to change the way it works.
   Strongly agree; Agree; Neither agree nor disagree; Disagree; Strongly disagree
7. The crisis, which occurred in the organization because of COVID-19:
   a. Disabled the organization's ability to continue operations.
   b. Affected negatively all areas of the organization's operations.
   c. Affected negatively some areas of the organization's operations.
   d. Affected negatively some areas of organization's but only at first.
8. The crisis, which occurred in the organization because of COVID-19 caused:
   a. No changes in the way in which organization is operating.
   b. The changing of the way of implementing everyday tasks but keeping the area of the organization's operations.
   c. The changing of the area of the organization's operations.
   d. Temporarily stopping the operation and resuming it only when the situation allows do it.

4 IT adaptability – research results

4.1 General remarks

The empirical research was performed to verify the mechanism of IT adaptability influence on organizational performance among organizations operating under conditions caused by BSE, including those which avoided a crisis caused by such conditions, those currently experiencing such crisis and those, which were not able to survive such crisis. The theoretical model, which was developed, was verified among those groups of organizations, showing the mechanism through which IT adaptability is influencing organizational performance.

The empirical research was performed among organizations operating in three different countries (Poland, the USA, and Italy) during the active wave of the COVID-19 pandemic. However, what is even more important, it was not the first wave. The research was conducted in the first quarter of 2021, which means that the COVID-19 pandemic already changed the business world due to introducing various countermeasures to delay and limit its spread, fostering the importance of IT support as the organizational resource, which enables the possibility to maintain business continuity under various critical conditions. It should be underlined that even though more than a year passed from the beginning of the COVID-19 pandemic and new "post-COVID19" business reality became to emerge, almost all organizations from the sample were still operating in crisis caused by the pandemic (only 90 organizations out of the sample of 1,206 reported that they are not currently in crisis). It should be noted that vast majority of them comes from Poland (50), while almost none organizations (9) reported such situation in the USA. Moreover, most of the organizations were operating in the second (338 organizations) and third (377 organizations) stages of crisis, showing threat they are currently actively preparing the response or responding to crisis caused by COVID-19 as the example of BSE, which occurred in the environment. It should be also noted that it is a case for every analyzed country.

The sample selection allowed to include in the sample organizations, which according to the control questions concerning the COVID-19 pandemic determined, that they were severely impacted by the pandemic and

DOI: 10.4324/9781003365044-5

the aftermath of its first wave, which caused them to redesign and reinvent the way they were operating in order to continue their operations. It must be underlined that the main aim of the research concerned the IT use in those organizations, therefore it became irrelevant from the point of view of this research to analyze whether organizations profited from the COVID-19 pandemic or lost their profit, as both those groups were forced to start using IT in much greater extent than before the pandemic.

4.2 IT adaptability positive influence on organizational performance

The regression analysis shows that the assumption found in the literature considering IT adaptability as a cornerstone, on which other IT characteristics are built in order for the organization to benefit from IT use may be indeed true. It seems that IT adaptability has the potential to influence organizational performance, regardless of the characteristics of organizations concerning Leavitt's model elements of organizations. It means that IT adaptability is statistically significantly influencing organizational performance in the model, which includes control variables, showing that regardless of the type of organizational structure, culture, technology, human capital, and goals, the influence occurs.

It allowed to conduct further statistical reasoning (through multigroup path analysis), identifying the mechanism through which IT adaptability influences organizational performance among three groups of organizations:

- Those which operate under critical conditions of BSE but are not in crisis.
- Those which operate under critical conditions of BSE and are in various stages of crisis.
- Those which have not survived crisis caused by BSE.

4.2.1 Organizations operating under BSE-caused conditions but not experiencing crisis

Among organizations operating in conditions caused by BSE but not experiencing crisis due to those conditions, the entire model is statistically significant and EDC-enabled IT adaptability is influencing organizational performance through organizational attitudes toward adaptable IT, employees' attitudes toward adaptable IT, IT reliability, and job performance (Figure 4.1). Moreover, the overall relations within the model are definitely the highest among this group of organizations. Especially the total effects of the influence of each element of the model on organizational performance are the highest (see Figure 4.2) and the mediating role of organizational attitudes toward adaptable IT and IT reliability are the highest among models calculated for each group of organization. It shows that IT adaptability may indeed be a cornerstone

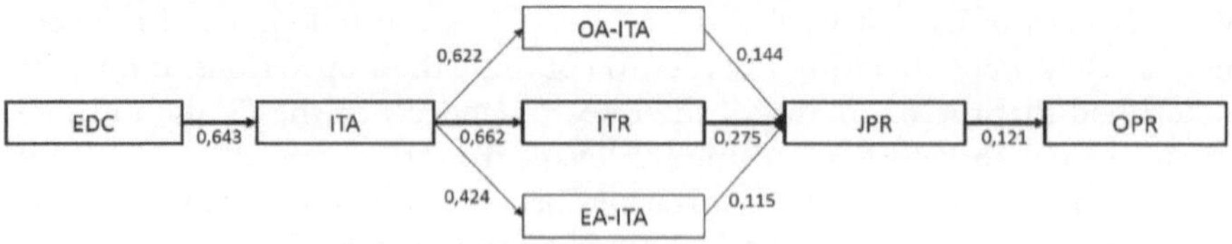

Figure 4.1 Organizations operating under BSE-caused conditions but not experiencing crisis

allowing organization to gain benefits from the use of IT on the level, which prevents them from experiencing the crisis. Of course, it should be stated that there are countless other variables which influence such preventions; however, the obtained models clearly show that IT adaptability is one of them. It should also be underlined that IT reliability is the strongest out of three parallel mediators in the model, showing that IT itself and its characteristics allow to translate adaptability into benefits for the entire organization among those, which are not experiencing crisis. Moreover, such well-grounded IT is supported by institutional-level solutions, as organizational attitudes toward adaptable IT is also an important mediator and individual-level attitudes as employees' attitudes toward adaptable IT also seems important. However, it should be vastly underlined that the strength of the relation between EDC and IT adaptability is also the highest among this organizations, which shows that EDC of employees indeed enables organization to gain benefits from IT adaptability and equips employees with skills specific for the proposed support of adaptable IT.

4.2.2 Organizations in the first stage of crisis caused by BSE

During the first stage of crisis, in which it is absolutely crucial to detect signals concerning the crisis, which may occur during BSE the situation is very specific, even though the entire model is statistically significant and EDC-enabled IT adaptability is influencing organizational performance through organizational attitudes toward adaptable IT, employees' attitudes toward adaptable IT, IT reliability, and job performance (Figure 4.2). In this case, employees' attitudes toward adaptable IT seems to be the strongest mediator out of three parallel mediators in the model, which further suggests that at the beginning of the crisis the role of employees is crucial. IT is not able to fully predict and detect conditions, which are threatening and have not happened before. The correct identification of such conditions as potentially threatening may be supported by IT adaptability, but the role of employees is especially important here. Therefore, the obtained results showing that indeed in this stage of crisis, the employees' attitudes toward adaptable IT is the strongest mediator, especially concerning the relation between employees' attitudes toward adaptable IT and job performance (te = 0.219 in

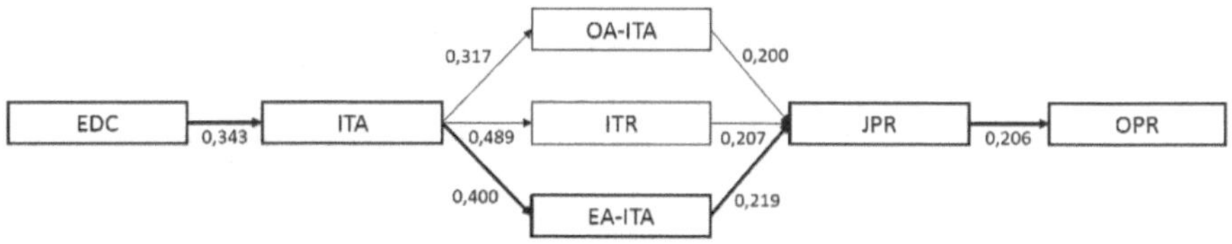

Figure 4.2 Organizations in the first stage of crisis caused by BSE

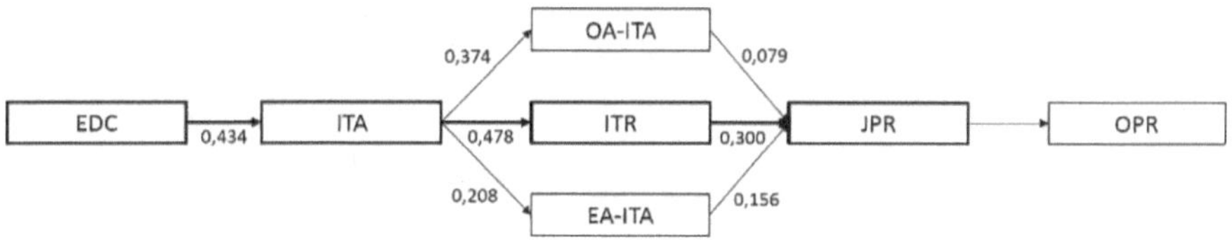

Figure 4.3 Organizations in the second stage of crisis caused by BSE

comparison to te = 0.200 and te = 0.207 for other parallel mediators) allow to contribute to the theory of crisis management in consideration with IT role in such for the first stage of crisis caused by BSE.

4.2.3 Organizations in the second stage of crisis caused by BSE

During the second stage of crisis, in which acute crisis is occurring and organization is starting to actively seek ways to battle such crisis, EDC-enabled IT adaptability is influencing only job performance, through organizational attitudes toward adaptable IT, employees' attitudes toward adaptable IT, and IT reliability (Figure 4.3). The IT reliability is the most important mediator out of three parallel mediators in the model. Moreover, even though the relation between IT adaptability and organizational attitudes toward adaptable IT is stronger than in case of employees' attitudes toward adaptable IT, it is different in case of their relation with job performance. In this case, employees' attitudes toward adaptable IT remains stronger showing that at this stage of crisis, individual attitudes seem to be more important than organizational ones. It may suggest that since general policies are not in place and organization is "doing their best" to analyze the situation and develop the response to the crisis, individual patterns of work and individual responses based on offered IT adaptability have more potential to influence organization as a whole. What's even more important is that this is the stage of crisis, in which job performance has no statistically significant relation with organizational performance, which means that organization as a whole is unable to gain any benefits from IT adaptability. It seems to be logical, as the fact that IT is adaptable is allowing organization to develop redesign and reconfigurations in order to fight the crisis, but they are not already in place.

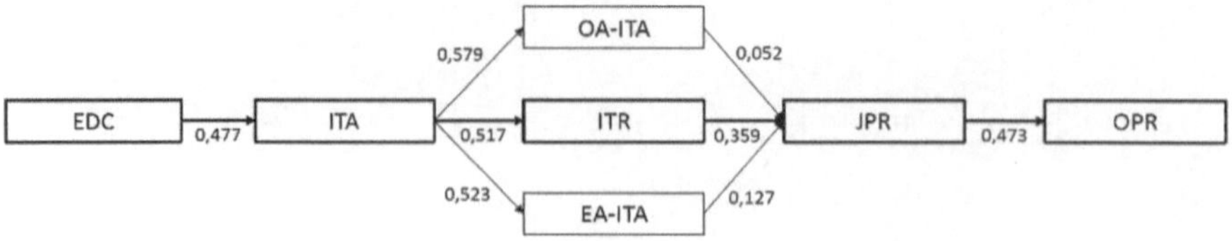

Figure 4.4 Organizations in the third stage of crisis caused by BSE

4.2.4 Organizations in the third stage of crisis caused by BSE

During the third stage of crisis, in which the chronic crisis is occurring but organization is already actively battling it, the entire model is statistically significant and EDC-enabled IT adaptability is influencing organizational performance through organizational attitudes toward adaptable IT, employees' attitudes toward adaptable IT, IT reliability, and job performance (Figure 4.4). However, the organizational attitudes toward adaptable IT seems to be the strongest mediator out of three parallel mediators in the model. It shows that redesign and reconfigurations already derived by the organization (through work of managers and their leadership) are slowly changing into institutional solutions (general policies and strategy) and it is what has the potential to strongly translate IT adaptability into the benefits for the organization as a whole. It shows that at this stage, individual approach of employees and IT characteristics are not that important and general (also often imposed) solutions developed by organization. However, what is important here is that in this critical stage of crisis, in which the organization is starting the battle to survive or collapse, all elements of the model are contributing to organizational performance, showing that the assumed relations are indeed true and significant for the organizations trying to survive he crisis.

4.2.5 Organizations in the fourth stage of crisis caused by BSE

During the fourth stage of crisis, in which the resolution is happening and the crisis is ending for the organization, not the entire model is statistically significant. EDC-enabled IT adaptability is influencing organizational performance only through organizational attitudes toward adaptable IT, IT reliability, and job performance (Figure 4.5). In this stage, organizational attitudes toward adaptable IT seems to be the much less important than IT reliability as a mediator out of three parallel mediators in the model. It shows that institutional solutions are in place and the reconfigurations already happened, which slows to conclude that all, which left to be done is to make sure that IT reliability will remain at high level after such reconfigurations and through that, the adaptability potential of IT translates into the benefit for entire organization. It should also be noticed that employees' attitudes toward adaptable IT seems to be statistically insignificant moderator in this case. It further confirms the fact that IT itself seems to be at most importance, supported by organizational-level at this stage and individual level is somehow following that lead and employees and their individual behavior is unable to substantially influence the main relation. Moreover, there is a strong relation between EDC and IT adaptability among organizations in this stage of crisis, which shows that the institutional solutions, which cased redesign and reconfigurations, may be used with success by employees equipped to handle changing conditions by their EDC.

4.2.6 Organizations which have not survived the crisis caused by BSE

Among organizations, which have not survived the crisis caused by BSE, the proposed model is not statistically significant and almost all the relations within the model are not statistically significant. In this group of organizations, EDC-enabled IT adaptability has the potential to influence job performance only trough IT reliability (Figure 4.6). It shows that indeed, IT adaptability is basing on EDC as its enabler (which further underlines the importance of such relation), however without the internal environment conducive for the use of IT adaptability (organizational attitudes toward adaptable IT and employees' attitudes toward adaptable IT) it is not possible to translate IT adaptability into the benefit for the entire organization. Such conclusions confirm once again that IT adaptability is one of the elements of organizations, which conditions the organization's ability to survive the crisis caused by BSE.

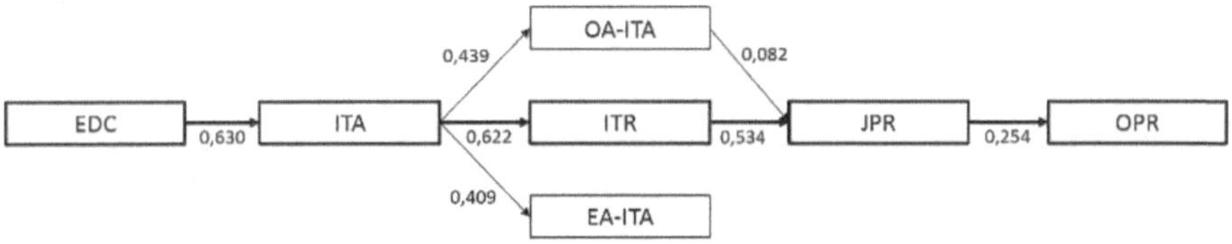

Figure 4.5 Organizations in the fourth stage of crisis caused by BSE

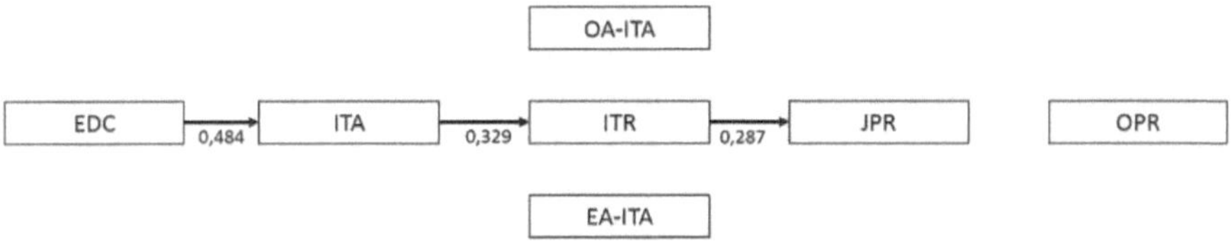

Figure 4.6 Organizations which have not survived the crisis caused by BSE

4.3 IT adaptability among organizations operating under conditions caused by BSE

The obtained results clearly show **that IT adaptability is an extremely important factor, which may very well be considered as a key for survival of organizations operating during crisis caused by BSE**. Such firm statement seems to be appropriate considering the shape of the model obtained for various groups of organizations.

The most important in this case are the results obtained for *organizations, which did not survive the crisis*. Among those organizations, there is no statistically significant influence of IT adaptability on organizational performance and its influence on job performance is very limited. It is existing only in case of IT reliability as a mediator of the relation and remains quite low. Comparing such findings with the shape of the model obtained for organizations, which are not in crisis, even though BSE occurs, or are fighting the crisis in various stages of its – it is indeed the biggest difference. In all of those models IT adaptability is influencing job performance through all three proposed mediators and in almost all of them, it is influencing organizational performance. Therefore, it remains in line with the view presented by Vahdat (2021), who assumed that "IT may become a boomerang for an entity if not managed effectively". The obtained results clearly confirm such statement and contribute to that, offering the additional information that IT adaptability, even coupled with IT reliability are not enough to avoid the boomerang effect. Without a proper support from the organizational and individual level, it is not possible to gain benefits for the entire organization. Such statement confirms that **IT adaptability should be treated as the key for survival of organizations operating under the conditions generated by BSE**. However, it should be enabled by proper competences of employees (EDC) and fostered by organizational-level, individual-level, and IT-level support in order for it to make a real positive impact on job and organizational performance.

Such statement is confirmed by models obtained for *organizations operating in various stages of crisis*. It remains clear that in every case the IT-level support is conducive for IT adaptability influence on organizational performance (through job performance). It allows to further develop the views of Asadzadeh et al. (2020), who stated that "the control of each phase of the crisis can be reached or facilitated using IT". Moreover, in most cases, the employees' attitude toward IT adaptability and organizational attitude toward IT adaptability has similar, although not that strong, role in the model. Wolff and Ladi (2020) are arguing that adaptive response is the most important step the organization can make during crisis caused by BSE. The performed research contributes new knowledge to that statement, underlining that IT adaptability is an important part allowing for such adaptive response. While analyzing the results obtained for each stage of crisis, it should be noted that the highest total effect of IT adaptability on organizational performance occurs in case of the third one. It definitely shows that IT adaptability has the largest potential to produce benefits for entire organization during the stage, in which actions are taken to contain the crisis based on developed solutions. It should be also stated that in this stage all three mediators (organizational-level, individual-level, and IT-level) are significantly boosting IT adaptability influence on organizational performance through job performance. It adds additional knowledge into the existing empirical evidence already offered in the literature, which indicate that IT support is useful in each phase of the crisis, particularly underlining its importance in the response phase (Reddick, 2011; Sakurai & Murayama, 2019; Tom-Aba et al., 2015). The added knowledge consists of the mechanism, through which that IT support is benefitting the organization: IT adaptability is influencing organizational performance through organizational attitudes toward adaptable IT, employees' attitudes toward adaptable IT, IT reliability, and job performance among organizations operating under crisis caused by BSE.

It should also be stated that the obtained results also allow to confirm **that IT adaptability is an extremely important factor allowing organizations not only to survive the crisis caused by BSE but avoid such crisis all together while operating under conditions caused by BSE.** Such statement is confirmed by the strength of the relations within the model, which are definitely the highest in case of organizations, which were not forced into crisis by BSE, which further confirm that the role of IT adaptability is important for shaping organizational performance among such organizations, supporting the initial hypotheses. It allows to confirm statements of Gronau and Rohloff (2007), who long before the COVID-19 pandemic stated that adaptable IT is crucial for any organizational transformations, which are inevitable in modern world to avoid crisis. The obtained results contribute new knowledge to that statement, offering insights concerning IT adaptability role among organizations operating under conditions of BSE, underlining that it may be a key for avoiding crisis all together, not only surviving it.

Therefore, the empirical research show that indeed, as summed by some authors, IT should evolve to be able to contribute for the organizational survival allowing for the best possible response to occurring crisis (Patrucco & Kähkönen, 2021). However, what's more important, such evolved IT (characterized by high level of IT adaptability) has the potential to benefit organizations in two ways:

- Support them in avoiding crisis caused by BSE.
- Support them in surviving crisis caused by BSE.

4.3.1 EDC as an enabler of IT adaptability

The obtained results allowed to confirm that it is not enough to support organization with IT during crisis caused by BSE. As stated above, they have shown that the IT must have adaptable nature. However, what is evenly important, such adaptable nature should be highly supported by a proper attitude of employees. Not only their EDC are important, enabling them to properly use adaptable IT and create synergy effect, which comes from combining their dynamic capabilities with IT adaptability, which concerns in a way dynamic capabilities of those technologies. Also, their attitude toward change within the organization caused, among others, by adaptable nature of IT, is important, as it allows such synergy effect coming from dynamic capabilities to transfer more strongly into job performance of employees, and then – performance of the organization as a whole. It is logical that employees, who have their dynamic capabilities developed more strongly, will have a natural tendency to be more open for changes occurring within the organization and much quicker in adapting to those changes. The role of EDC as an enabler of IT adaptability is significant in every analyzed group of organizations. However, it should be underlined that that relation is especially strong (comparing to different stages of crisis) in the fourth stage of crisis: resolution. It shows that as mentioned before, during this stage of crisis all the solutions are already in place and IT is already reconfigured to match the changes needs of the organization and the EDC becomes especially important as it allows employees to function properly in such redesigned organization. Moreover, it should be underlined that even among organizations, which have not survived the crisis, the EDC is showing the potential to enable IT adaptability. It is not enough, as due to other reasons such enabled IT adaptability is not translating into organizational performance; however, the relation between EDC and IT adaptability is still confirmed.

Therefore, the research allowed to **further develop the theory concerning dynamic capabilities of employees**, stating that EDC has the key role in enabling IT adaptability in organization. It seems that IT itself (without a proper support from employees equipped with specific competences) cannot generate as much benefit for organization as IT properly enabled by employees with high levels of EDC.

4.4 IT adaptability boosters

The obtained results allow to confirm the main assumptions that there are three levels of organizational functioning, which have the potential to influence the level of benefits, which can be gained by the organizations from the adaptable IT support, which is the most important conclusion offering **contribution to the field of IT management, especially during crisis**. Those levels concerned: institutional-level (organization as a whole), individual-level (employees as an element of that organization), and IT-level (IT as area of organization under the study). It was indeed confirmed that all of them mediate the relation between IT adaptability and organizational performance (through job performance) among organizations operating under conditions of BSE, both in and not in crisis. It allows to confirm that following assumed mechanisms are truly in place for translating IT adaptability into organizational performance: on the institutional-level – shaping organizational strategy, policies, and culture conducive for the use and support of IT adaptability, which is achieved through managers work and leadership; on the individual level – shaping employees' attitudes to foster the use and support of IT adaptability, which is achieved through their individual patterns of work and self-leadership; on the IT-level – shaping IT characteristics in a way, which allows to maximize to possibility of use of its adaptable features, which is achieved through IT reliability.

What's especially interesting is that the level of IT seems to be the strongest mediator among the three of them in most cases (including lack of crisis and lack of ability to survive it). However, two cases in which it is different are also utmost importance for the organization.

4.4.1 Organizational attitude toward IT adaptability (institutional-level)

The obtained results allow to confirm the views of Rowold and Abrell-Vogel (2014), who indicated that the most important facilitators of changes within the organization are indeed managers. The commitment of managers and their own perspective and willingness to adapt to any changes has the possibility to influence the employees. The performed empirical research allowed to confirm such statement in case of IT adaptability and managers' capabilities to foster its proper use in organization. The role of organizational attitude towards IT adaptability has shown to be important in case of all crisis stages. Indeed, it was not the strongest mediator and remained rather in the background for IT reliability and employees' attitude towards IT adaptability; however, it can be said that without it, it would not be possible to obtain proper levels of those other mediators, which finally translate into higher organizational performance obtained due to IT adaptability. Even though compared to other mediators, organizational attitudes toward IT adaptability was usually the weakest, it should be underlined that its role is the most important in case of the first stage of crisis, during which it is a key to be able to detect signals of crisis, which will be caused by BSE and prepare for the analysis and development of redesign of the existing IT support. It shows that indeed it all starts with the organization as a whole, in which managers start acting to initiate process, which further on allow organization to properly use their adaptable resources (including IT). It offers a **contribution to the field of study concerning crisis management**, showing the need for including the possible mediation of organizational-level variables while analyzing the role of IT support during crisis.

4.4.2 Employees attitude toward IT adaptability (individual-level)

The role of employees attitude toward IT adaptability, which is mixed with their ability to enable such adaptability show that the mediation of individual-level variables is even more important. The obtained results in this case allow to offer strong **contribution into the field of study concerning leadership in crisis** and the role of managers during the course of it. As underlined by Marques-Quinteiro et al. (2019), not only leadership but also self-leadership is important in case of crisis occurring within the organization, especially during rapid and unpredictable changes connected to BSE. The results confirmed that EDC-enabled IT adaptability is influencing job and organizational performance through both of those lenses: organizational attitude toward fostering adaptability, which is connected to leadership and the role of managers within the organization, and employees' attitude toward fostering adaptability, which is connected to self-leadership. Hence, the obtained results allow to confirm that there is a need to broaden our understanding of contemporary leadership, including the self-leadership perspective and observing the growing importance of employees own decisions and their role for the organization as a whole. It allows also to further develop the assumptions of Yue (2021), who stated that leadership is not enough for organizations operating under critical conditions of BSE, especially in the new digitalized environment which is enabling employees to work from home and is giving them much more independence. He underlines the need for including the perspective of employees' commitment to changes, especially from the point of view of their attitudes toward the adaptability. It seems that those results, which confirm the need to shape the support for IT adaptability with both lenses: organizational and individual one, are especially important not only from the perspective of management practice but also the theory development in the context of leadership. It seems that those lenses strength in mediating the relation between IT adaptability and organizational performance (through job performance) is changing through various stages of crisis; however, they are both needed and important.

Moreover, the results confirm the views of Kumar et al. (2021), who stated that reliable IT influences job performance due to the increasing employees' organizational commitment and job satisfaction because of its ability to boost their motivation. It connects to the fact that employees are aware of poorer possibility for performing their work and by contributing (sometimes more than usually) without any control they feel more independent, responsible, and committed, hence their performance is rising. Analyzing the role of employees' attitude toward IT adaptability and organizational attitude toward IT adaptability, together with IT reliability as the three mediators of the relation between IT adaptability and organizational performance and their role in boosting such performance through the performance of employees (job performance), it seems that those assumptions not only were true, but even underestimated the role of employees and their commitment towards the organization (including the use of adaptable IT in it). It seems to be an important **contribution to the field of human resource management** in the context of IT use, as it shows a kind of a double loop – fostering IT adaptability may have a positive influence not only for organization as a whole but also individual employees and their performance, but fostering such adaptability is impossible without the engagement of those employees in the process. The employees themselves (both in case of their capabilities and attitudes) have the potential to foster the influence of IT adaptability on their performance and the performance of the organization as a whole.

It should be underlined that the role of employees attitudes toward IT adaptability it the strongest in case of the first stage of crisis, during which employees are becoming a key resource in organization, which is able to detect signals of crisis, which will be caused by BSE and their commitment to redesign the existing IT support and use existing IT adaptability into their own and the organizational advantage may be a source of great competitive advantage for organization entering the crisis, driving its possibility to survive it.

4.4.3 IT reliability (IT-level)

Based on the work of Tworek (2021) and Martono et al. (2020), it was assumed that adaptable IT is not enough if employees are not prone to use it, as they are not convinced that the adapted IT is still reliable and will produce results allowing them to fulfill their tasks with the benefit for the organization as a whole. The role of employees as both enablers and boosters of IT adaptability influence on organizational performance was discussed in detail above. However, it should be firmly underlined that their value would be impossible to contribute when IT itself is not reliable enough for them to willingly use it. The obtained results fully confirm such views, as IT reliability is the strongest mediator of the relation between IT adaptability and organizational performance in almost every group of organizations. In case of all the models obtained for each stage of crisis, IT reliability is a significant mediator of the relation between EDC-enabled IT adaptability and organizational performance. It allows to form the following conclusions concerning its role for contemporary organizations:

- IT reliability allows organization to achieve benefits from IT adaptability.
- IT reliability allows organization to boost their benefits from IT adaptability because of positive attitudes of employees, who are willing to properly use it.
- IT reliability allows organization to fully utilize EDC as an enabler of IT adaptability.

Such conclusions allow to contribute the **new body of knowledge in the field of IT management, especially in the context of IT reliability**.

The role of IT reliability was not discussed in detail in the context of organizational crisis (especially caused by BSE); therefore, the obtained results are important, as they allow to fulfill the research gap, which exists in this regard.

References

Asadzadeh, A., Pakkhoo, S., Saeidabad, M. M., Khezri, H., & Ferdousi, R. (2020). Information technology in emergency management of COVID-19 outbreak. *Informatics in Medicine Unlocked*, 21, 100475.

Gronau, N., & Rohloff, M. (2007). Managing change: Business/IT alignment and adaptability of information systems. *Proceedings of the Fifteenth European Conference on Information Systems*, ECIS 2007, St. Gallen, Switzerland.

Kumar, P., Kumar, N., Aggarwal, P., & Yeap, J. A. (2021). Working in lockdown: The relationship between COVID-19 induced work stressors, job performance, distress, and life satisfaction. *Current Psychology*, 40(12), 6308–6323.

Marques-Quinteiro, P., Vargas, R., Eifler, N., & Curral, L. (2019). Employee adaptive performance and job satisfaction during organizational crisis: The role of self-leadership. *European Journal of Work and Organizational Psychology*, 28(1), 85–100.

Martono, S., Nurkhin, A., Mukhibad, H., Anisykurlillah, I., & Wolor, C. W. (2020). Understanding the employee's intention to use information system: Technology acceptance model and information system success model approach. *The Journal of Asian Finance, Economics and Business*, 7(10), 1007–1013.

Patrucco, A. S., & Kähkönen, A. K. (2021). Agility, adaptability, and alignment: New capabilities for PSM in a post-pandemic world. *Journal of Purchasing and Supply Management*, 27(4), 100719.

Reddick, C. (2011). Information technology and emergency management: Preparedness and planning in US states. *Disasters*, 35(1), 45–61.

Rowold, J., & Abrell-Vogel, C. (2014). The influence of leaders' commitment to change on the effectiveness of transformational leadership in change situations – a multilevel investigation. *Journal of Organizational Change Management*, 27(6), 900–921. doi: 10.1108/JOCM-07–2012–0111.

Sakurai, M., & Murayama, Y. (2019). Information technologies and disaster management–Benefits and issues. *Progress in Disaster Science*, 2, 100012.

Tom-Aba, D., Olaleye, A., Olayinka, A. T., Nguku, P., Waziri, N., Adewuyi, P., … & Shuaib, F. (2015). Innovative technological approach to Ebola virus disease outbreak response in Nigeria using the open data kit and form hub technology. *PloS one*, 10(6), e0131000.

Tworek, K. (2021). IT reliability for ensuring performance of IT used in organizations operating under Covid-19 epidemic crisis. *Central European Business Review*, 10(1), 39–53.

Vahdat, S. (2021). The role of IT-based technologies on the management of human resources in the COVID-19 era. *Kybernetes*, 51(6).

Wolff, S., & Ladi, S. (2020). European Union responses to the Covid-19 pandemic: Adaptability in times of permanent emergency. *Journal of European Integration*, 42(8), 1025–1040.

Yue, C. A. (2021). Navigating change in the era of COVID-19: The role of top leaders' charismatic rhetoric and employees' organizational identification. *Public Relations Review*, 47(5), 102118.

5 Conclusions

The main aim of the monograph was to verify the mechanism of IT adaptability influence on organizational performance among organizations operating under conditions caused by BSE, including those which avoided a crisis caused by such conditions, those currently experiencing such crisis, and those which were not able to survive such crisis. Such aim was fulfilled through systematic literature review, which provides a basis for the development of the theoretical model of IT use in contemporary organizations, and empirical studies which allowed for the verification of such model.

The assumed aim was achieved, which led to the fulfillment of identified research gap by proposing a theoretical **model of EDC-enabled IT adaptability influence on organizational performance** and its empirical verification among organizations operating under conditions caused by the COVID-19 pandemic (as an example of BSE).

The literature review allowed to assume that contemporary world, which emerged after the beginning of the COVID-19 pandemic, differs significantly from the one in which organizations were operating before the pandemic. First, the level of digitalization, which was forces by the circumstances related to limiting and delaying the pandemic spread, fundamentally changes the role of IT in contemporary organizations. They were forced to rely on this type of technology to much greater extent, and its proper use became a necessity. Moreover, its improper and inefficient use became a reason for lack of ability to maintain business continuance. Second, the pace and diversity of changes occurring in the environment became unprecedented, forcing organization to operate in massively turbulent and dynamic environment, in which BSE happen much more often and organizational crisis may become a new normality for business world, with one changing to the other.

Based on that, it was assumed that there is need for developing a new approach for the analysis of IT in organizations operating in such new business world. The previously known approaches have not accounted for many circumstances, which are characterizing current IT use patterns. In light of that, IT adaptability was presented as a one single cornerstone, which may be one of the strongest sources of the contemporary organizations ability to benefit from IT use.

DOI: 10.4324/9781003365044-6

Building on that and showing the significance of adaptable IT support and the role of organizational support for its use (both on the systemic and individual level), the idea behind the new approach for analyzing IT in organizations emerged. The literature analysis allowed to formulate following assumptions concerning organizations operating in new digitalized, turbulent business world, often under conditions caused by BSEs, which were a basis for the model development:

- EDC (capabilities of individual employees) is enabling a proper use of IT adaptability.
- IT adaptability is influencing organizational performance through job performance of employees (characteristic of individual employees).
- IT adaptability is influencing organizational performance through mediators from three levels of organizational support: institutional-level (organizational attitudes toward adaptable IT), individual-level (employees' attitudes toward adaptable IT), and IT-level (IT reliability).

Based on the performed literature review, it was visible that tremendous shift in the business environment of contemporary organizations (which happened due to the COVID-19 pandemic) indeed called for the redefinition of the role and importance of IT support, and literature reviews confirmed its key role in maintaining organizational operations and its survival.

The empirical results allowed to confirm the assumptions formulated based on the literature review and reasoning performed based on that. The empirical study performed among 1206 organizations operating in Poland, Italy, and the USA during an active wave of the COVID-19 pandemic allowed to formulate a vast set of conclusions useful not only from the point of view of management theory development but also from the point of view of utilitarian use.

It is important to underline at the begging that the results showed that organizations are indeed slowly beginning to operate in the "day after" environment, which differs significantly from the world known from before the COVID-19 pandemic and is currently an everyday challenge for contemporary entrepreneurs. First, level of dependence on IT support among studied organizations is very high, showing that it became a necessity to use those technologies. Second, there is a much higher level of turbulence of environment and its unpredictability, which is indeed causing various BSEs to occur more frequently than before, which easily force organizations into crises. Almost all organizations out of the examined sample (1206) have declared that they experienced more than one BSE, which significantly influenced their operations.

Organizations are still either trying to avoid a crisis or experiencing various stages of it due to turbulence of environment caused by the COVID-19 pandemic itself. The sample contained 1,206 organizations, out of which 90 were not in crisis and significant amount of them not survived the crisis.

Hence, the majority of organizations are operating in various stages of crisis. Such conclusion is underlining the importance of the study and the conclusions coming from it.

Moreover, the results allowed to formulate the following conclusions concerning the mechanisms of IT support for contemporary organizations:

- IT adaptability has the potential to support organizations in avoiding crisis caused by BSE.
- IT adaptability has the potential to support organizations in surviving crisis caused by BSE.
- Lack of IT adaptability may contribute to the collapse of the organization due to crisis caused by BSE.

Such conclusions allow to confirm that IT adaptability is indeed a cornerstone for IT support in contemporary organizations, determining that without the properly developed and maintained possibility to adapt existing IT into rapidly cad unpredictably changing conditions, it is very hard to maintain the continuity of functioning of contemporary organizations. Such adaptability is considered to be the added value allowing organizations to maintain and strengthen their organizational performance under conditions of the growing need for IT use on a daily basis connected with the unprecedented turbulence of the environment. First, it allows to maintain the continuous alignment between IT and organizational needs, positively influencing the perceived reliability of such IT and allowing employees to better utilize their employees' dynamic capabilities. Second, it allows to improve the job performance of employees through that mechanism, joined with the conducive effect of supporting internal environment (organizational and employees' support towards adaptability). Moreover, the research allowed to confirm that IT adaptability itself is not enough, as it must be supported by conducive environment within the organization, which will:

- enable proper IT adaptability use through EDC,
- foster IT adaptability use within the organization.

Fostering IT adaptability use should be nurtured on three levels:

- on the institutional-level – shaping organizational strategy, policies, and culture conducive for the use and support of IT adaptability, which is achieved through managers' work and leadership,
- on the individual-level – shaping employees' attitudes to foster the use and support of IT adaptability, which is achieved through their individual patterns of work and self-leadership,
- on the IT-level – shaping IT characteristics in a way, which allows to maximize the possibility of use of its adaptable features, which is achieved through IT reliability.

Therefore, the monograph proposed new theoretical model indicating the factors related to adaptable IT support and determining their role in enabling and fostering positive influence of IT adaptability on organizational performance of contemporary organizations. It is assumed that IT adaptability enabled by EDC influences organizational performance through organizational attitudes toward adaptable IT, employees' attitudes toward adaptable IT, IT reliability, and job performance. Such theoretical model was empirically verified on the sample of organizations operating under the conditions of active wave of the COVID-19 pandemic in Poland, Italy, and the USA, using multigroup path analysis.

Such designed and empirically verified model provided a basis for theory development in the field of IT management, organizational continuity, and reliability during crisis caused by BSE and leadership, offering the new body of knowledge related to the factors boosting organizational performance related to IT, establishing it as one of the main resources enabling organizational survival under such conditions. They also allowed to contribute to the theory development in the field of IT management itself, determining that IT adaptability must be enabled and fostered on three levels: individual (which is at most importance in case of enabling IT adaptability with proper competences of employees), organizational, and IT.

At the same time, the model has the utilitarian importance, as it will allow to propose conclusions and mechanisms to be used by contemporary organizations to gain more benefit from IT support and enable their higher performance under changed conditions of functioning – digitalized and more IT-dependent world, with significantly higher dynamics and unpredictability of the environment.

Index

Note: **Bold** page numbers refer to tables and *italic* page numbers refer to figures.

AAA capabilities 54, 58
Abrell-Vogel, C. 68, 117
Aceto, G. 11
acute crisis stage 29, 88
adaptability: defined as 53; notion of 59
adaptive performance 70, 72, 75
Adaptive Structuration Theory (AST) 17
Agenda for Sustainable Development 10–11
agility 58
Ahsan, M. 58
Aldunce, P. 35
Almutairi, A. 55, 61
Alpaslan, M. C. 23
Alsahli, S. F. 62
Amoroso, D. L. 17
anticipated usefulness, defined as 18
Aprianingsih, A. 21
Asadzadeh, A. 114
assembly line 6
AST *see* Adaptive Structuration Theory (AST)

Bailey, J. E. 17, 18
Bernard H. 14
Bessant, J. 14
Beynon, D. 53
Bieńkowska, A. 74
Black Swan events (BSEs) 1, 2; COVID-19 as example of 31, **32,** 33; COVID-19 pandemic, understanding IT support after 39–40; crisis in IT 35–38; IT adaptability during 57–59; model development 122; organizations operating in first stage of crisis 110–111, *111*; organizations operating in fourth stage of crisis *112,* 112–113, *113*; organizations operating in second stage of crisis 111, *111*; organizations operating in third stage of crisis 112, *112*; as specific type of crisis 26–31
Black Swan event stage 27, 28
"The Black Swan. The Impact of the Highly Improbable" (Taleb) 26
Boin, A. 70
Boland, R. J. 56
Burrell, D. N. 73

Campbell, J. P. 72
capability, defined as 77
Carbonara, N. 13
Cetindamar, D. 14, 15
Chakravarthy 58
Chan, S. L. 7
Cheney, P. H. 17
Chen, S. W. 40
Chou, T. C. 40
chronic crisis stage 29, 88
Comfort, L. K. 34
Computer-Assisted Web Interview (CAWI) method 87
Confirmatory Factor Analysis (CFA) 90
control questions 106, 108; COVID-19 107; Leavitt 106–107
conventional crisis 24
Coombs, R. 28
Coordinating Systems 13
Cotec, P. 14
COVID-19 pandemic 1, 62, 108, 121; on contemporary organizations 1–2; as example of Black Swan event 31, **32,** 33; IT after 39; IT during crisis, caused

by BSE 35–38; in Poland, Italy, and USA 3, 86, **87,** 124; understanding IT support after BSE 39–40
crisis 105–106; characteristics of 24; defined as 22; IT adaptability, model in 77; leadership in 118; perspectives of 22–23; stages of 88; typologies of 23–25
crisis-as-event perspective 22, 26, 27
crisis-as-process perspective 22–23, 26
crisis, caused by BSE 26; management in various stage 30–31; research perspective 26–28; stages of 28–30
crisis, IT in 33; caused by BSE 35–38; Resource Based View 33–34
crisis management processes 30–31, 117
Cronbach's α 90

Davis, F. D. 17
Davison, C. 36
DeLone, W. 21
DeLone, W. H. 20, 21–22
DePietro, R. 17
DeSanctis, G. 17
Deverell, E. 69
Diffusion of Innovations Model (DOI) 16
digital business transformation 40
digital competences 11
Digital Education Action Plan (2021–2027) 10, 11
digitalization, level of 121
Dogson, M. 14
DOI *see* Diffusion of Innovations Model (DOI)
Donthu, N. 31
Dwivedi, Y. K. 31

ease of use, defined as 18
ECS *see* Enterprise Collaboration Systems (ECS)
EDC-enabled IT adaptability 97, 101, 109–113, 118, 121, 124
EIS *see* Executive Information Systems (EIS)
empirical research 108; multigroup path analysis 91–100; Phase I 86; Phase II 86; regression analysis 90–91, **91**; research methodology 86–87, **87**; research results description 100–101; sample selection 87–88, **88**; variables (scales reliability and validity) 88–90, **90**
employees' attitudes toward adaptable IT (EA-ITA) 89, 103, 118–119; as booster *70,* 70–72; relation between IT and 75
employees dynamic capabilities (EDC) 73–74, *74,* 89, 102; as enabler of IT adaptability 115; influence on IT adaptability 75–77; work-related attitudes 74–75
Enterprise Collaboration Systems (ECS) 13
Executive Information Systems (EIS) 13
Exploratory Factor Analysis (EFA) 90

Falletta, S. 62
Fink, S.: four-stage model 28, 30
"5P" 11
five-stage model 30
Fleischer, M. 17
four-stage model 28, 30
Foxall, G. R. 22
fully adapting organizations 69
fundamental crisis 25

Ghandour, Ahmad 55
Goodhue, D. L. 17
Green, L. W. 19
Gregory, M. J. 15
Groenewald, D. 55
Gronau, N. 55, 58, 75, 115
Gundel, S. 23, 24
Gustafsson, A. 31

Han, J. H. 55
Heart, T. 54, 68, 69
Henderson, J. 9
Hermann (1963) 22
Hirschheim, R. A. 21, 56
Hobday, M. 14
Huang, J. L. 70, 72
human information processing 34
human resource management 119
Hutchby, I. 17

IBM SPSS AMOS software 90, 91
Ifinedo, P. 63
individual-level organizational functioning 64, 118–119, 123
information reliability 65, 67
information technologies (IT) 1, 6; acquisition and implementation stage 15–16; adoption models 16–20; crisis (*see* crisis); definition of 6–8, **7**; exploitation stage 16; identification stage 15; importance for organizations 8–12; life cycle 14–16; new model need for use 20–22; perceived usefulness support 10–12; preservation

and learning stage 16; quality of information 20; quality of support services 20; quality of system 20; selection stage 15; typology 12–13
infrastructure 55
institutional-level organizational functioning 63, 117, 123
intractable crisis 25
IS Success Model 60
IT adaptability (ITA) 3, 89, 102–103; boosters 116–117; boosters influence on organizational performance 63–72; during BSE 57–59; dimensions of 56, **57**; EDC as enabler of 73–77, *74,* 115–116; emergence of COVID-19 pandemic 52; employees attitudes toward *70,* 70–72, 118–119; influence on organizational performance 52, 121; ISO/IEC 25010 norm 55; IT reliability 119–120; job performance and organizational performance *59,* 59–63; levels of 123; mediated influence on organizational performance 72–73; model in crisis 77; notion in organization 54; organizational attitudes toward 67–70, *68,* 117; organizations operating under conditions caused by BSE 114–116; positive influence on organizational performance 109–113; relation between IT reliability and 93–96
IT-business alignment 9–10, 54
IT deployment 9
IT dynamic capabilities 54; defined as 77
IT-level organizational functioning 64, 119–120, 123
"IT monarchy" 34
IT reliability (ITR) 64–65, 89, 104, 119–120; as mediator 65–67, *66*; relation between IT adaptability and 93–96
IT success model 20

Janssen, M. 58, 59
Jin, J. 14
job performance (JPR) 59, *59,* 89, 104; defined as 60; IT adaptability influence on organizational performance through 60–63; mitigation of negative effects on 66
job satisfaction 75
Jundt, D. K. 70, 72

Kabra, G. 63
Kähkönen, A. K. 58
Knowledge Management Systems 13
Koronis, E. 53
Kreuter, M. W. 19
Kukafka, R. 19
Kumar, P. 118

Ladi, S. 114
Leavitt, H. J. 6
Leidner, D. E. 33–34
Levin, D. Z. 14
Lippényi, Z. 67
literature coverage: to crisis management and IT 33; of issue of IT-business alignment 10; IT support during COVID-19 **38**; of role of IT reliability 65
Liu, D.Y. 40
Luftman, J. 10
Lu, J. 75
Lu, W. 20
Lyytinen, K. 21

Management Information Systems (MIS) 13
Mann, R. I. 17
Maoz, H. 54, 68, 69
Mardiana, S. 21
Marques-Quinteiro, P. 61, 118
Martono, S. 119
Masthoff, J. 53
McKinsey Global Institute 8–9
McLean, E. R. 20–22
Mercedes, D. 73
Milasi, S. 39
MIS *see* Management Information Systems (MIS)
Mitroff, I. I. 23, 28, 30
multigroup path analysis, organization model 91; in first stage of crisis caused by BSE 92–94, **93, 94**; in fourth stage of crisis caused by BSE 97–99, **98**; not survived crisis caused by BSE **99,** 99–100, **100**; in second stage of crisis caused by BSE 94–96, **95**; in third stage of crisis caused by BSE **96,** 96–97, **97**; without crisis but under BSE conditions 92, **92, 93**
Murayama, Y. 35

Nadikattu, R. R. 39–40
Naim, M. 55
National Science Center, Poland 86
Ngo-Ye, L. 58
non-adapting organizations 69

Okanga, B. 55
Olsson, E. K. 69
Operational Support Systems (OSS) 12–13
organizational attitudes toward adaptable IT (OA-ITA) 89, 104, 117
organizational crisis, components of 22; *see also* crisis
organizational functioning: individual-level 64, 73; institutional-level 63, 73; IT-level 64, 73; levels of 63, 73
organizational performance (OPR) 59, *59,* 89, 105; boosters influence on 63–72; defined as 60; IT adaptability influence on 121; IT adaptability influence through job performance 60–63; IT adaptability mediated influence on 72–73; IT adaptability positive influence on 109–113; mitigation of negative effects on 66
organization-based perspective 55, 56
organizations: attitudes toward IT adaptability as booster 67–70, *68*; differences between three groups of 101; in first stage of crisis caused by BSE 110–111, *111*; in fourth stage of crisis caused by BSE *112,* 112–113, *113*; groups of 69; operating under BSE-caused conditions but not experiencing crisis 109–110, *110*; in second stage of crisis caused by BSE 111, *111*; in third stage of crisis caused by BSE 112, *112*; which not survived crisis caused by BSE 113, *113*
OSS *see* Operational Support Systems (OSS)
Otrachshenko, V. 33

Pallister, J. G. 22
Pan, G. 33–34
Pan, S. L. 33–34, 38, 39
Paramythis, A. 53
Patrucco, A. S. 58
PCS *see* Process Control Systems (PCS)
Pearson, S. W. 17, 18
Persico, V. 11
person-job fit 74
Pescapé, A. 11
Petter, S. 21
Phaal, R. 14, 15
Pisano, G. 74, 77
Pitt, L. F. 20
PLC *see* programmable logic controller (PLC)
Pliskin, N. 54, 68, 69
Ponis, S. 53
Poole, M. S. 17
Post-Black Swan event stage 27, 28
post-COVID-19 business 2–3, 108
Pre-Black Swan event stage 27–28
PRECEDE model 19
Probert, D. 14, 15
Process Control Systems (PCS) 13
Process Systems 13
programmable logic controller (PLC) 6

RBW *see* Resource Based View (RBW)
realignment model 58
regression analysis 90–91, **91,** 109
research gap 2
resolution stage 29–30, 88
Resource Based View (RBW) 33–34
Rogers 16
Rohloff, M. 55, 58, 75, 115
Roux-Dufort, C. 26
Rowold, J. 68, 117
Roztocki, N. 8
Rumsfeld, Donald 26
Rush, H. 14

Sakurai, M. 35
SAM *see* Strategic Alignment Model (SAM)
SCOT *see* Social Construction of Technology Model (SCOT)
Seddon, P. B. 20–22
self-leadership 71–72, 117, 118
semi-adapting organizations 69
Shepherd, D. A. 33
Shoss, M. K. 70, 72
Shuen, A. 74, 77
Sisodia, G. 60
situational theory 69
Social Construction of Technology Model (SCOT) 16
Soja, P. 8
Solis, B. 40
Stewart, G. L. 71
Stewart, R. A. 14
Strategic Alignment Model (SAM) 9
Sumanth, D. J. 14
support service reliability 65
Sustainable Development Goals 11
Sutcliffe, K. M. 53
system-based perspective 55, 56
system reliability 64

Taleb, N. N.: "The Black Swan. The Impact of the Highly Improbable" 26
TAM *see* Technology Acceptance Model (TAM)
Task-Technology Fit model (T-T Fit) 17
TAT *see* Technology Affordance Theory (TAT)
Technological Industry 4.0 11
Technology Acceptance Model (TAM) 16–22, 66
Technology Affordance Theory (TAT) 17
technology management (TM) 14
Technology-Organization-Environment Framework (TOE) 17
Teece, D. J. 74, 77
Thompson, R. L. 17
three-stage model 28
Tjakraatmadja, J. H. 21
TOE *see* Technology-Organization-Environment Framework (TOE)
Transaction-Processing Systems (TPS) 12–13
triggering event 23
T-T Fit *see* Task-Technology Fit model (T-T Fit)
Turner, M. 21
Tworek, K. 64, 65, 74, 119

Ubaidillah, E. 71
unexpected crisis 24–25
Unified theory of acceptance and use of technology (UTAUT) 17, 20–22
usage reliability 64–65
UTAUT *see* Unified theory of acceptance and use of technology (UTAUT)

Vahdat, S. 36, 59, 114
value-creation 55
Van Der Lippe, T. 67
Van Der Voort, H. 58, 59
Venkatesh, V. 17
Venkatraman, N. 9
Vogus, T. J. 53
Von Zedtwitz, M. 14

Wanasida, A. S. 61
Wang, S. 8
Wang, Y. 55
Warner, J. 7
Weibelzahl, S. 53
Weisboard Six Box organization model 62
Weisbord, M. R. 62
Weistroffer, H. R. 8
Whisler, T. L. 6
Wiarda, E. 17
Williams, T. A. 30, 33
Winter S. G. 77
Wolff, S. 114
work engagement 75
work motivation 75
work-related attitudes 74–75
Worline, M. C. 53

Xu, J. 20

Yousafzai, S.Y. 22
Yue, C. A. 71, 118

Zeng, M. 75
Zhang, S. 38, 39